# PRAISE FOR SUB-LEBRITY

"A ribald romp [through the] 'very out' queer [world ...] it draws readers [...] one level, always spicing its writing with flamboyant descriptions that are notable for their engrossing observations and personal flair ... especially highly recommended for aspiring performing-arts participants"

Diane Donovan, Senior Reviewer
*Midwest Book Review*

"An exciting and heartfelt adventure ... lighthearted, humorous, and inspirational ... Acord immediately hooks readers with his personable, approachable, and candid tone. Humor and comedy play a big part in his book ... he treats the reader like a friend, and injects tidbits of wisdom, advice, and self-reflexivity throughout ... Acord curates his life events to create a cohesive narrative ... and clearly has a strong understanding of how to craft successful narratives"

Zahrah Ahmad
*AvidBards*

"Acord shares his story with wit and good humor ... a vividly written memoir, one which pulls the reader in"

David-Elijah Nahmod
*Bay Area Reporter*

"Filled with dish, honesty, and laughs ... If you have ever had a dream that you were afraid to follow, you need to read this"
*Reviews by Amos Lassen*

"Unflinchingly honest ... clever and engaging ... Acord is not afraid to lay it all out there"
Sarah
*All The Book Blog Names Are Taken*

"Vividly written with refreshing candor"
*South Florida Gay News*

Dishy but heartfelt ... the most fun I've had during quarantine"
Manny the Movie Guy
NBC Palm Springs

"Funny and poignant, at times graphic, and very, very honest"
Anthony Corona
*Take 2 Radio*

EXPLETIVES **NOT** DELETED

Also by Leon Acord

*SUB-LEBRITY\* The Queer Life of a Show-Biz Footnote*

# EXPLETIVES NOT DELETED

## LEON **ACORD**

LARILEE ENTERTAINMENT • LOS ANGELES

*Expletives Not Deleted*
Copyright © 2014, 2020, 2021, 2023 by Leon Acord
All rights reserved

No part of this book may be reproduced or transmitted in any form or by any manner whatsoever without written permission of the author, except in the case of brief quotations embodied in critical articles and reviews. For information, address laurence@odnt.tv.

This is a work of nonfiction. The names and identifying characteristics of some of the individuals featured throughout this book have been changed to protect their privacy.

ISBN 9798449228505

First Edition

Larilee Entertainment, Culver City, California

Cover photo: Norman A. Palley

*For my parents
Judy & Norm,
with much love & deep gratitude
(sorry for all the naughty words)*

## Acknowledgments

"I Didn't Choose to Be Gay, but…" first appeared on Huffington Post on November 24, 2014, in a slightly different form.

"10 Reasons to Embrace Aging Gaily" first appeared on Huffington Post on Oct 22, 2014, in a slightly different form.

"Why Do We Love Divas? Let Us Count the Ways" first appeared on Huffington Post on November 11, 2014, in a slightly different form.

"Closets Are for Costumes" first appeared on Huffington Post on October 29, 2014, in a slightly different form.

"My First Plague" first appeared on Huffington Post on December 3, 2014, in a slightly different form.

"Breaking In, Changing Channels" first appeared on LeonAcord.com on September 27, 2020, in a slightly different form.

"On Cancel Culture" first appeared on LeonAcord.com on March 4, 2021, in a slightly different form.

"Fuck Facebook" first appeared on LeonAcord.com on October 25, 2021, in a slightly different form.

"Why Wonder Woman?" first appeared on LeonAcord.com on October 10, 2021, in a slightly different form.

"A Twisted Vein" first appeared on LeonAcord.com on September 19, 2020, in a slightly different form.

## Contents

Portrait of the Artist as an Old Fart  1

The First Bite  5

I Didn't Choose to Be Gay, But...  9

Breaking In, Changing Channels  13

10 Reasons to Embrace Aging Gaily  27

Unsolicited Parenting Advice from a Childless Know-It-All  31

On Cancel Culture  35

Essential Film-Viewing Guide for Today's Young Gay Male  39

From Black to Worse  57

Fuck Facebook  63

Where There's Smoke, There's Ire  71

Secrets of a Successful Long-Term Relationship?  87

Why Do We Love Divas? Let Us Count the Ways  95

Why Wonder Woman?  99

Blond on *Blonde*  105

Tech Kills: A Partial Casualty List  111

Closets Are for Costumes  119

Critical, Darling  123

My First Plague  133

A Twisted Vein  139

Am I a "They"?  145

Sub-lebrity Auction  151

Worry *and* Be Happy!  161

# Portrait of the Artist as an Old Fart

I've been trying very hard lately to *not* become a grumpy old queen.

I fear I'm not being entirely successful.

Much of my failure is due to things most of us experience as we segue into "senior citizen" status. Many bodily functions we took for granted in our 20s, 30s, and 40s now require attention, focus, and sometimes even some coaxing.

I can no longer eat everything I want to eat, or smoke with abandon (or at all). Red meat? Ha! The boundless energy I used to enjoy? Gone with the wind. My vision is shot. My lower back is a mess. I have nerve damage in my right hand. A large blind spot in my right eye. An occasionally retracted ear drum in my left ear. A piriformis sprain in my right hip. Insomnia. Anxiety. Allergies. Dry eye. Eczema.

I used to take pride in never needing meds. Those were the days! I now take anywhere between four and eight pills (depending on how many of the above-listed ailments are acting up) before I go to bed. My husband Laurence and I also take multiple supplements. Between the two of us, we have so many prescription drugs and vitamins that we utilize the thin slide-out cabinet in our kitchen, clearly designed for use as a spice rack, to house our many bottles of tablets and capsules.

I used to hope to die without pain. Now I realize, by a certain age, one can't even *live* without pain. We can only hope to die with dignity. Dignity? There's a first time for everything!

Remember sex? I barely do! (Of course, I've been married for thirty-plus years, so that *might* have something to do with it…)

When I look in the mirror these days, I see my parents looking back at me. I've never had Botox or any other injectables, nor any surgeries, to "freshen up" my face. But despite being pretty religious about skin care, I'm finding there's only so much that over-the-counter products, avoiding direct sunlight, and washing your face every night can do. My face is slowly sliding down the front of my skull.

Yep, getting older is a fucking ball of laughs … but it sure beats the alternative!

The irony is, back when I was running from audition to audition, performing on stage most weekends, and holding down a day job (at least most of the time), I'd fantasize about what life would be like when I turned 60. I thought I'd happily be willing to downsize my life. I expected I'd be ready to relax into my golden years. I just *knew* I'd embrace a "smaller" existence.

Ha! After 25-plus years of an active career – including five years of hyperactivity with *Old Dogs & New Tricks*[1] – inactivity can still make me a bit nuts, even as I crave it.

---

[1] The streaming sitcom I created, wrote, and starred in (about four middle-aged gay friends in West Hollywood) from 2011-2016. You can watch it on Prime Video or Gay Binge TV.

And even if getting older were a breeze, it's not particularly reassuring to approach retirement age as Republicans desperately try to raid the funds we all paid into Social Security. They undermine our democracy. They inflict their hypocritical ideas of a "religious" nation on those who don't share their ideology. They enable the causes of global warming in the name of capitalism and profits. They refuse to budge on common-sense gun legislation. They ignore science, the rule of law, common decency. They …

There I go again. Grumpy old queen.

On second thought, I have every reason to be grumpy.

Lately, there's not enough time to process *today*'s outrages before *tomorrow* provides new reasons to be furious. So what one writes today can read like old news by tomorrow; by week's end, it's a distant memory; and it's completely forgotten in a year.

Simultaneously, time also feels as if it's standing still these days. (Trump *still* hasn't been indicted?[2] COVID is *still* around?) In many ways, we're living the same reality every single god-damned day.

How does one capture, in words, what it means to be alive *right now*, when life itself moves at both the speed of sound *and* at a snail's pace?

How do I write about modern life without it reading like "yesterday's news" tomorrow?

How do I complain about current annoyances and fears *without* sounding like a grumpy old queen?

---

[2] Sing hallelujah! Trump was finally indicted, by the State of New York for his hush-money payments to porn star Stormy Daniels, just as this book went to press. May it be the first of many!

In 1946, in an essay entitled "The Prevention of Literature," George Orwell wrote that totalitarianism makes literature – fiction, non-fiction, journalism – impossible. He wrote that totalitarianism isn't something just restricted to corrupt regimes or countries – societies in which "groups of people who have adopted a totalitarian outlook" were just as deadly to literature. (Hello, MAGA!)

Orwell warned of a potential future with "a schizophrenic system of thought, in which the laws of common sense held good in everyday life and in certain exact sciences, but could be disregarded by the politician, the historian, and the sociologist."

Wow. Forget *1984*. George could've written *2020*. And it's two sequels, *2021* and *2022*.

If I don't at least *try* to reach readers outside my own "bubble," am I merely contributing to that "schizophrenic system of thought"?

Fuck it. Guilty as charged.

I'll try to keep the didactic lecturing to a minimum and throw in some fun bits here and there.

Because, honestly. If Billy Joel were writing *We Didn't Start the Fire* today, he'd have a nervous fucking breakdown.

# The First Bite

I can't remember a time when I didn't want to be an actor. But that ambition had lots of competition early on.

Being a typical Gemini, I also wanted, at various times, to be a ventriloquist, a circus clown, a comic-book writer, a magazine editor, a newspaper reporter, a private detective, a homesteader, a cowboy, and a superhero.

But all those other dreams and goals died a quick death in eighth grade, when the theatre bug "bit" me.

Ironically, I was nowhere near a theatre when I was bit. It was in a social-studies classroom at Maconaquah Middle School in Bunker Hill, Indiana, where I first became afflicted.

At the beginning of the school week, Mr. Berger told our class that on Friday, we would be reading a short play out of our textbooks – something about a Chinese family saved by their pet turtle.[3] He would be assigning roles to be read to members of the class.

*Pick me! Pick me! Pick me!* That was the only thought running through my brain as Mr. Berger assigned roles to select students. And I was thrilled when the teacher asked me – *me!* – to read the role of the father. I mean, come on, it was the "starring" role, after all!

---

[3] I really wish I could remember the title, or more about this play, given its importance in my life!

For the first time, my acting ambition not only kicked in, but into high gear, no less. I decided I would *memorize* my lines (*just like real actors do!*) instead of just reading them, and thus impress my teacher with my talent, skill, and determination. After all, every actor on TV memorizes his or her lines. Just how hard could it be?

I soon learned, *very hard!*

But I refused to give up. Over the next three days, I kept trying. And trying. And trying.

Homework? Who has time for that? *I'm an actor!*

When simply reading the text over and over didn't do the trick, I recorded the lines onto a cassette tape, and played them back while I slept at night. (If only memorizing lines could be done so easily – alas, there are *no* shortcuts!)[4]

By the time Friday rolled around, I had given up on being "off book." But otherwise, you'd think I was about to open on Broadway. I was excited, scared, determined. *Will sixth period ever get here?* I couldn't wait to get through my other classes.

Finally, it was time. I was surprised to find I was shaking with stage fright, but as I would do for decades to come, I channeled it into positive energy.

I even tried to emulate a Chinese accent. Yes, a farm boy in Indiana, trying to sound Asian. Good Lord. Thank God smartphones were still science fiction in the late 1970s, or else I would *still* be in hiding!

---

[4] Here's how it's really done: You repeat your first line, over and over and over. Then, you add the second line, and say them both repeatedly. When you have those two lines down, you add the third, and repeat and repeat and repeat. Not very glamorous, is it?

Somehow I got through the reading. Near the end, as "Dad" talks about how the turtle saved his family, I was struck with an inspiration. I gently stroked the plastic prop turtle on its head – and the class burst out laughing!

No, it wasn't a comedy. Yes, I inappropriately "pulled focus" from the story and my "cast mates." What would you expect? I was a virgin. It was the first (but not the last) instance of my being an undeniable "ham."

At the end of the reading, the class applauded.

Then Mr. Berger said, "I bet we're going to see Leon's name up in lights on day!"

And that was that. I was a goner.

# I Didn't Choose to Be Gay, But...

The other day, a friend and I were discussing the ridiculous notion that being gay is a choice rather than a biological disposition. He asked, "What man would choose to be gay? Being straight is so much easier!"

I thought about that for a moment. *Is it?* Knowing what I know now, I realized that if we *did* get to pick the team on which to play, I wouldn't hesitate to choose the team that I am on.

When you're gay, you're an outsider from day one, before you even admit it to yourself.[5] You are outside society looking in, and that particular vantage point is not to be dismissed. This changes your outlook on everything. You don't buy the party line. You question convention. You can react instead of being the stoic straight guy.

You accept all shades of gray in society with little to no judgment because you know that most societal misconceptions are just that: misconceptions.

When I was growing up on the farm, there was an unspoken assumption that I would get married shortly after high school, join Dad in the fields full time, move into one of the houses on

---

[5] Granted, I'm writing from the prospective of a 60-year-old man. Things have gotten easier for subsequent generations, but it does remain a struggle.

the property, have kids to help out, become a partner in "Acord Seed Farms," and that would be that.

Once I came out to my parents, those expectations died a very quick death.

I no longer felt the pressure to buy into the "American dream." There were no expectations for me to get married, have 2.5 kids, and support my family. I didn't have to follow all the rules society imposes on straight guys.

But it still wasn't easy. There was bullying and name calling, which gave me a thick skin and a talent for enduring conflict. I realized very early on that the taunts said more about the bullies than about me. I wondered whether it was possible that these bullies were actually, in a subconscious way, envious that I could so easily opt out of the "gender games" in which they were stuck.

I could access my "feminine side" with no conflict. I understood concepts that most straight guys dismiss as nonsense.

These days, with over half a century behind me, I now question whether things are truly "easier" for straight boys and men in our society. Most gay men, sooner or later, get over caring about what others think. Straight men, on the whole, seem to spend their entire lives worrying about it.

Consider this: Yes, straight men rule the world, but it isn't all beer and pretzels. Society projects expectations onto straight men to be strong, silent, and long-suffering. You're supposed to put your own life on hold while you have kids (whether you want them or not) and labor to support your family. You're supposed to dress simply, without imagination.

Straight men aren't supposed to show much emotion.[6] Yet their wives want them to do just that.

Straight men are expected to follow sports. Love cars. Know how to fix everything around the house. They're expected to kill the spider in the bathroom. Open the jars. Shovel the snow. But if you actually enjoy spending time with children, if you cry, you are suspect.

If you don't get married, you're selfish. Or a player. Or a Peter Pan who refuses to grow up.

Yet for some reason, people don't expect gay men to "grow up." We're allowed, if not expected, to be unconventional, creative, artistic, well-spoken, well-groomed, well-dressed. We can be artists. Nowadays we can even be so butch, so "normal," that folks wouldn't guess we're gay. In fact, now we can even follow straight folks' lead and get married and have children ourselves.

There's also more freedom in terms of career choices. I worked as a male secretary in my 20s in San Francisco, and it didn't raise an eyebrow. We're no longer surprised to see men in professions that used to be reserved just for the ladies: teacher, flight attendant, nurse, nanny. You straight guys can thank us queens for that!

Yes, gay men still have our own set of challenges. But save your pity for straight men. I'm happy. I'm gay. I'm happy I'm gay. And I wouldn't have it any other way.

---

[6] Again, things are getting better for straight men. How do I know? Since my "gaydar" no longer works, many straight dudes seem totally gay to me now!

# Breaking In, Changing Channels

Given my status as a minimally successful actor, I'm always surprised whenever someone asks me, of all people, for advice on how to break into show business.

Back in the dark ages, I'd tell them to do what I *didn't*. That is, enroll in the best liberal-arts college you can, get the finest theatre training available, and don't even *think* of auditioning for anything (other than school productions) until after you get that theatre degree!

I no longer offer that advice. I know lawyers and CPAs who struggle to pay off student loans despite stable, high-paying careers. Advising kids to rack up a ton of debt for a career in the arts? That now feels foolhardy, if not downright reckless.

These days, I tell them to do what I *did*: Read plays and autobiographies of actors. Find an affordable, high-quality acting class led by a teacher with whom you really connect. Study for at least four years straight before you start submitting yourself for roles.

And then, stay put for a while. Get as many acting credits as possible on your resume (and scenes on your demo reel). Submit to student films. Audition for community theatre. Write and produce your own shows and short films.

And then – but only then – you can think about moving to a more-competitive "show-biz capital" like Los Angeles or New York.

Because while it's great to be a big fish in a small pond, those towns are vast oceans where only the sharks survive.

But which city? That depends on you.

If you can sing and dance as well as act, I'd recommend New York City.

If you're drop-dead gorgeous, you should probably head straight to LA.

If you are an identifiable "type" – cop, lawyer, terrorist – lucky you! If you're an odd duck like me, you're going to have to create many of your own opportunities.

"Then what?" they ask.

"Don't wait for the phone to ring. Use that video camera on your phone! Use YouTube and other venues to share your creations!"

"But then what?"

"Beyond that, I got nothing," I reply.

I took over six years off from pursuing other gigs to focus on writing and acting in the streaming TV series *Old Dogs & New Tricks*. Once my show posted its final episode, I returned to an industry I now barely recognized, and I still have trouble adapting to what the business is now.

Show biz *never* stops changing.

The latest changes have been radical, and in the past decade, even more wildly so, thanks to game-changing technology and COVID.

"Present day" is no longer "present" tomorrow. So I really can't offer further present-day guidance.

But I *can* whine about how it has changed. Can't I? *Please?*

Let's begin at the beginning, with the way most journeyman actors land a majority of their roles. The audition.

Until very recently, the process went like this:

After reviewing your resume, headshot, and maybe your demo reel, a casting director ("CD") would call to schedule an appointment. She'd either email you the scene you'd be reading, or she'd tell you where to find it online.

You'd leave early enough to ensure you'd be on time, traffic be damned. During your drive, you'd run the scene, do vocal exercises, think of real-life emotions you might incorporate.

You'd park your car. The adrenaline would be rushing, but much like being called to "places" before a play, you'd transfer that nervous energy into *positive* energy.

Once inside, you'd sign in and say hello to the receptionist. You'd take a seat in the holding area. Very often, other actors were there, waiting to read for the same role, so you could "size up" your competition. Many of them you'd have seen before, in other waiting rooms at other auditions.

When you were called in to audition, you'd quickly "read the room." Was the CD and her staff laidback and chatty? Had you auditioned for this CD often enough that she remembered you? If so, you might indulge in just a (very) little back-and-forth conversation before the reading.

But if you sensed they were no-nonsense, humor-deprived, or perhaps short on time, you'd display your professionalism and get right to the work.

You'd stand on your mark, slate (state your name and representation, show your profiles, etc.) to the camera, and then begin the scene.

They might have given notes – an "adjustment" – and asked you to do it again. You'd think, *hooray!* because now you can show them some range and how well you take direction.

Then, unless they asked you to confirm your availability, you'd offer a "thank you" and exit the room with no small talk, as that can come across as kiss-assy.

Meeting you in person gave them a feeling of what you were like, and what you'd be like to work with. And vice versa.[7]

Sometimes, when you were very lucky – or really right for the part – you'd even get a feeling that "Hey, I may actually get this part!" as you left.

And as you walked to your car, you could let it all go.

But – *uh oh!* – if you found yourself replaying your audition over in your head while driving home, chances are good that you hadn't done your best work. In that case, you'd stop for a cheeseburger, to have a drink, to buy sleazy underwear – whatever would help you let it go and return to real life.

There is a lot to be said for that old-fashioned way. There's something about knowing you have only this one chance to do the absolute best work you can do, just one opportunity to make a good impression. It feels a bit daredevil-esque, like doing theatre, and I think it inspires many actors to do their best work.

---

[7] More than once, I've left an audition thinking, "I wouldn't work with those assholes even if they *did* cast me!"

I once met Bryan Cranston, shortly before he found mega-fame with *Breaking Bad*. He gave me the best advice about those old-time in-person auditions. He said he never saw them as "job interviews." Instead of handwringing over his chances of getting the part, he focused only on the actual work, and appreciated and relished the opportunity to perform. That's it. Because in reality, on a film set, you rarely get to act for more than a few minutes at a time, just like doing an audition!

I loved his approach and emulated it myself – until it all completely turned to shit.

Thanks to technology, in-person auditions are now as dead as Kanye West's career. Casting directors realized they no longer needed to spend money on rent. Or cameras. Or office staff. Not when they can pass the burden and expense onto the actors!

Nowadays, actors are expected to tape our auditions at home and submit them electronically.

Now, I hate even taking selfies. But if one wants to work, one does what one must.

Over time, some CDs have become increasingly demanding about the quality of those self-taped auditions. These days, an invitation to submit frequently comes with very detailed instructions:

"Against a solid white background, do a full-body slate. Then walk into a close-up shot and turn so we can see both profiles and the back of your head. Then, in separate video files, walk into a head-and-shoulders shot and give us two different takes of each of the four scenes we've sent – and label each file with your name, the project name, and the date."

An LA actor no longer needs just talent and a car to audition. (Somewhat good news, considering gas prices these days!) In addition to talent, he or she must now have:

- A laptop or smartphone
- A high-quality ring light
- Lighting skills
- A sound-proof room[8]
- A large backdrop or blank white wall with no photos, posters, or artwork
- A high-quality microphone
- A teleprompter (for dialogue-heavy scenes)
- A reader (someone to read the other role(s))
- A digital voice recorder (in case you don't have a reader)
- Patience
- Time
- Someone to distract the cat

Forget acting classes. Now there are classes to teach actors how to create high-quality self-tape auditions. An entire side industry of equipment and instruction has been born.

But at what price? No longer will you get a sense of whether they liked what you did. You don't even know if they watched what you did at all!

Gone are opportunities to establish and build face-to-face working relationships with casting directors. Gone is the

---

[8] A necessity in Los Angeles, where the soothing sounds of sirens, helicopters, and leaf-blowers are omnipresent.

chance to create chemistry and the chance to size up the other "contestants" you're playing against.

The biggest loss, though, is that marvelous *one-and-done, one-chance-to-nail-it, feels-like-theatre* adrenaline rush. Nowadays, you can shoot take after take (after take after take after take). You can spend all morning recording, all afternoon deciding "which ones?" and then even more time editing, labeling, and submitting the files.

Shop for sleazy underwear afterwards? Ha! Your evening is spent breaking down the equipment and putting away your at-home casting office. And finally paying attention to your howling cat!

Actors aren't the only ones sold short in this new system. I believe it does a disservice to the casting directors, as well.

It's a lot like dating via Zoom. Can one really get a sense of chemistry, or of a person's true energy, if you can't see body language, or smell pheromones? How can one notice "the little things" if you're locked into a head-and-shoulders shot with a fancy ring light, a soft-focus filter, and a created background?

After dating that someone on Zoom, how many might still be disappointed when meeting that person in person?

It makes me nostalgic for the days of being stuck in traffic.

Poor little me, huh? Enough bellyaching about my troubles! Let's broaden our scope and look at how the industry itself has morphed during my time in the trenches – starting with television.

TV had already changed drastically since the 1970s when it first inspired me to be an actor. We went from three major networks to *hundreds* of channels!

Advances in the past decade alone are mind-boggling. When we first launched *Old Dogs & New Tricks* in 2011, Amazon was still just a place to buy books and CDs. Netflix was still in the DVD-mailer business.

Today, every company short of Waffle House has its own "network." Streaming services Netflix, Hulu, and Amazon Prime now dominate the Emmys as HBO once had (and CBS had before that). Several major studios have launched their own streaming services.[9] Those poor "legacy" networks, as they're now called, are becoming antiques, desperate to stay on our radar.

Literally hundreds of shows, limited series, and movies come and go. It seems impossible to keep up with so many series and films, harder still to accomplish "market penetration." Small, loyal audiences are now just as impressive to advertisers as casual large audiences. Forget broadcasting and trying to attract tens of millions of viewers. "Narrowcasting" is now the name of the game, and a smaller, very devoted following is just as desirable.

There is a plus side. Once the bastard stepchild of Hollywood, the TV industry is now more respected than the feature-film industry. (And COVID only served to further blur the lines and cripple cinemas, but that's another rant!)

On the down side, it's harder than ever for unknowns to break in.

When I grew up watching TV, there was a stable of journeyman actors, respected in the industry but otherwise unknown – actors you'd vaguely recognize in the supermarket

---

[9] How many streamers will actually survive remains to be seen.

without remembering from where. They made their careers by guest-starring on series TV, season after season.

Today, with *so many* former "names" also scrambling for work, those one-and-done episodic guest roles now go to these once-famous faces. This is often called "stunt casting" and it gets ratings. (I know, I've done it myself while casting *Old Dogs*.) And it's moved everyone down a rung or three on the show-biz food chain.

Let's move on to the big picture – literally. The movies.

Growing up, I loved gritty, small character-driven films of the 1970s. When I began my career in the 1990s, thanks to Sundance and little movies like *She's Gotta Have It* and *Sex, Lies & Videotape*, independent film was thriving. And so were the markets for those films.

Art houses. Film fests. Midnight movies. Home video. All thrived in the 1980s and 1990s.

But *now?* Going. Going. Gone. Gone.

Now you might sell a small film to one of the streaming platforms, but don't expect to recoup production costs unless your film somehow catches fire and lands you a deal for future films.

As for big studio movies, because they're now so expensive and bloated with superheroes, space battles, epic special effects, and over-the-top gore, the big studios must also eye the global market to make that money back. That means they want films with as much action and as little dialogue as possible (so much for character-driven films). And thanks to those zany Chinese, all – and I mean *all* – references to

LGBTQ characters and lifestyles are – well, how do you say "absolutely forbidden" in Mandarin?

Let's face it. If forced to choose between the millions of dollars to be made in Asia, versus showing diversity, which do you honestly think Hollywood is going to choose?

It's "Don't Say Gay!" on a global scale.

Perhaps the biggest alteration in the show-biz fabric of our modern world is social media.

To stay relevant, stars *and* wannabes must post constantly: fabulous photos on Instagram, witty political bytes on Twitter, upcoming appearances on Facebook, clips from talk shows on YouTube. And there are other apps, like TikTok and Twitch, that this old fart has no knowledge of!

Producers and casting people don't want actors now. They want "influencers." To them, the number of followers someone has is often as important as the amount of talent s/he offers – sadly, sometimes *more* important. It often makes the difference between who gets the part and who doesn't.

Some young "actors" make serious mint not by starring in some sitcom or releasing a hit song, but by simply posting photos of themselves in some pseudo-glamorous setting, drinking this energy drink, or wearing those sneakers, or checking into that hotel – all provided at no charge by the manufacturers of those products if the influencer's numbers and engagements are high enough.

There's a reason your favorite A-list movie stars are lining up to star in TV series on cable and streaming, and not just because the quality now exceeds that in films, or because the seasons are usually much shorter than those on "legacy" network shows.

In today's *blink-and-the-conversation's-moved-on* era of total media saturation, hundreds of networks, and dozens of streaming venues, stars (and agents and managers) realize that starring in one big-budget film every 12-18 months is no longer enough to stay in the *zeitgeist* longer than a week or two. By then, everyone will be talking about the *next* big thing. New product is needed constantly to keep fans engaged and talking, and one needs to be in as much product as possible to make that happen.

It's all too exhausting to think about!

My husband tells me I'm a better actor now than I've ever been. And he's right. After a lengthy career – and particularly following five years of playing *Old Dogs'* neurotic Nathan Adler – I have serious chops. My emotions are fluid. I no longer require much "prep time" to deliver the goods.

The irony is, I've never had fewer opportunities.

I used to believe, if I kept acting into my 60s and 70s, many of my contemporaries would eventually give up or retire (or even die), and the competition would become far less steep. What I failed to consider is, as one ages, there are fewer and fewer roles for which to compete!

Diversity casting, a wonderful change long overdue, has also limited my opportunities. Until just recently, any role in which race wasn't an issue was, by rote, mostly offered to white actors. That is increasingly no longer the case, thankfully. Actors of color are finally getting more and more opportunities, which delights the (selfless) liberal in me – even if it sometimes frustrates the (selfish) actor in me!

After over 60 roles in theatre and films and a successful series, I also find I'm now far less inclined to chase after parts. Most actors are *starving* for work. I've been blessed to have spent many happy years gorging at a buffet.

I haven't given up. I can still produce my own projects. And I love it when friends and colleagues ask me to appear in their projects, as I did recently in Bruce Hart's comedy feature *OPEN*, and Destiny Fletcher's play *Valentine's Last Dance*.

And yes, God damn it. When I see that rare casting notice that really sparks my interest – or rarer still, when agent Belinda submits me for something – I will begrudgingly drag out all the equipment, turn on all the lights, transform the bedroom back into an at-home casting office, lock the cat in the guest room, and tape that fucking audition!

Another reason I'm picky about what I chase after?

I was spoiled rotten by working with a thoroughly prepared and professional cast and crew on *Old Dogs & New Tricks*. It's much harder now to bite my tongue when new colleagues don't match the professionalism of my former long-term team.

Case in point:

Huddled in a shadowy North Hollywood storefront to avoid the blistering 90-degree sunshine, actor Wenzel Jones and I waited for our extremely late theatre director to show up for rehearsal. When said director arrived, some twenty-plus minutes later, he informed us he'd lost the keys to the theatre.

We'd have to rehearse up on the roof, he said, until the theatre owner showed up.

"I am not rehearsing on the roof in this heat!" I snapped. "I expect my director to be inside the theatre, waiting and ready to start rehearsal on time. Why should we care about being punctual if you don't?"

Rightly cowed, the director scrambled off mumbling apologies. Feeling instantly guilty, I turned to Wenzel.

"Why can't I be one of those actors who can go off on a director without immediately feeling bad afterwards?"

"There's a name for actors like that, Leon," Wenzel deadpanned. "They're called 'stars.'"

One thing I know: I am not, never have been, and never will be a "star." And I'm quite happy with my obscure status as a moderately successful sub-lebrity!

# 10 Reasons to Embrace Aging Gaily

Chances are, if you are a gay man "of a certain age," you feel a wide range of emotions about it – and not a lot of them good. You may feel rejected by gay society or ignored by the younger generations coming up. Or you might fear becoming one of those gay men who ignore the clock and keep living a lifestyle that no longer works for them.

What if I told you that there are just as many compelling reasons to celebrate "aging gaily"?

Once you stop laughing, hear me out…

Like the changing seasons, each stage of life has its pluses and minuses. In autumn, you can complain about the cold wind and the shorter days – or you light a fire, enjoy the vibrant fall colors and look forward to Halloween and Thanksgiving!

It's all a matter of tweaking your thinking. For every reason to feel like life as you know it has ended, there is an equally compelling reason to embrace your age. It's just a matter of perspective.

The next time you feel depressed about your age, remind yourself of these ten advantages of "aging gaily." I guarantee you will feel better!

1. You realize that speaking your mind is empowering. You no longer play games. You no longer present a false self to "fit in." You know who you are, and you don't try to change to please others. If some don't accept you for who you are, you

shrug it off and move on, because you know there are plenty who will. They don't call them the "Fuck-You Fifties" for nothing!

2. You've had enough "sport sex" and now recognize it for what it is. You don't read more into it. And if you're seeking more than sport, you change your tactics. You've been around long enough to know true love almost never happens on Grindr.

3. You've seen gorgeous men age badly, and other men actually get better looking with age. You realize that looks are ever-changing. You're not as likely to fall for just a pretty face or a hot body. (I've looked 35 since junior high. Now that I've "grown into" – and then even "outgrown" – my face, people tell me I look younger than my age for the first time ever!)

4. Patience. You finally learn that good things are worth the wait.

5. In the 70s, it was the Communists. In the 80s, it was nuclear holocaust, and the Japanese takeover of our economy. Then it was Islamic terrorists and Ebola. The media has always predicted the end of the world. When you stick around long enough, you learn to take *most* of the dire warnings with not a grain, but a *boulder* of salt.

6. Friends become family. You learn the true meaning of family – a group of people who love you, warts and all. You don't have to be uncomfortable, keep secrets, or hide your authentic self from this new family.

7. Speaking of friends, when you go to bars now, it's to celebrate with friends, not to look for sex. (Ironically, not looking for sex makes you even more desirable!)

8. You no longer tolerate toxic friendships. You recognize people who enhance your life and eliminate those who don't.

9. You learn not to beat yourself up about mistakes you've made in life. Instead, you look for the lessons, vow not to make the same mistakes twice, and then keep going.

10. Most importantly, we survived AIDS! We've lived long enough to see gay marriage become a reality! Those are reasons enough to celebrate! (Especially since a lot of our peers weren't so lucky.)

Much like coming out, there's nothing to lose and everything to be gained by embracing your age.

So stop complaining about the cold wind and shorter days. Pull on a heavy sweater, have a pumpkin latte, and enjoy your autumn.

# Unsolicited Parenting Advice from a Childless Know-It-All

Let's be honest. No kid wants to be best friends with his or her (or their) parents before the age of 30. And rightly so.

It goes against nature. Moms and dads who resist centuries of basic human behavior to attempt being "besties" with their offspring are ripping the very fabric of society. You should be your kids' boss and benefactor, but *not* their best bud.

This trend has been going on for a few decades now. I can't tell you exactly when parents began going "soft." But I have a couple of theories as to why.

Here's one: It *is* human nature for parents to want to provide their kids a life "better than we had." Perhaps these parents, already pampered a bit themselves as kids, feel they must now up the ante and spoil *their* children even more.

Here's another: Maybe it's not really about helping kids avoid the painful moments and difficult lessons that come with growing up. Maybe it's the parents who don't have the fortitude to endure the pain when little Dylan doesn't get a trophy, or when young Sophia loses that spelling bee. Maybe Ma and Pop are sparing their own feelings, avoiding their own discomfort, by ensuring every child gets a trophy, win, lose or draw. If Aiden and Chloe still get prizes for merely showing up, they won't have a meltdown on the way home. Mom and

Dad can avoid an uncomfortable car ride. Hell, they can avoid testing their parenting skills altogether.

I don't want to paint a portrait of *my* parents as hard and unfeeling because that definitely was not the case. They were very proud of both of us, they wanted to us succeed, and they hated it when we didn't. But win or lose, my sister Tammy and I either *won*, or we *lost*. There was little sugar-coating of reality in the Acord household.

That's because Norm and Judy knew that losing once in a while was important and unavoidable. (And that made winning, to us, all that much sweeter.) They knew losses were life lessons. There was no "pep talk" when I failed to get the part in that first school play. I didn't go to them when I was being bullied for being gay. Extravagant birthday parties weren't annual events, but rather, were saved for the "big" birthdays like 10 or 16 – and even then, they weren't all *that* grand. Candles but no pyrotechnics!

And when we screwed up? No pampering then, either.

"You play, you pay," was one of Dad's favorite admonishments.

Believe me, I have my own assortment of hang-ups and neuroses.[10] But thanks to my parents, I take responsibility for my actions. I know how to "take a punch" without always falling to pieces. And when I *do* fall apart, I know it's up to me to pull myself back together again.

Unfortunately, this is not so true for too many of today's young adults.

---

[10] After reading this far, you probably don't need to be told.

However it happened, some young Americans are so easily bruised by life's bumpy road, they should be encased in bubble wrap.

Case in point:

My husband recently hired twenty-something "Lisa" at his restaurant. On her third day of work, and without so much as an email or phone call, she strolled in over an hour late without apology.

"Uh, Lisa, you're an hour late. What's up with that?" he calmly asked her when she finally arrived.

"Oh!" Lisa appeared absolutely stunned at first, then burst into tears as she stammered, "I assumed your company had a grace period!"

*A grace period? Of an hour?* For fuck's sake!

Ironically, while many parents no longer have the resolve to share difficult, painful losses with their children, they have become more emboldened to lash out at anyone who dares to suggest their brats aren't winners.

For example, high-school sports and little-league baseball teams across America are cancelling games due to umpire and referee shortages.

This is due to increasingly unhinged – and sometimes even violent – outbursts from parents at games. Nobody wants to risk a punch in the face for simply declaring little Jacob or Isabella struck out!

By the way, what a *wonderful* example to provide for our children, as we verbally attack or physically pummel others for simply stating the hard truth!

So, what do we get when younger generations face no consequences, and no discomfort without first receiving a "trigger warning?" When we raise kids to believe what they want is all that really matters? When we give them the message that "getting" something is far more desirable than "working for" something? When they see their parents blaming others for their children's failures?

You get people like Matt Gaetz, that's what. Marjorie Taylor Greene. Lauren Boebert. "Pharma bro" Martin Shkreli. Theranos' Elizabeth Holmes. WeWork's Adam Newman. And too many online "Karens" to count.

Repugnant, unrepentant, spoiled brats all.

So if you're a new parent, stop trying to make your children's lives uninterrupted bliss. For God's sake, stop trying to be your kid's friend. They aren't here for that. They are here to be embarrassed by you. Occasionally, they're even supposed to hate you. Deal with it. Endure it. And hang out with people your own age!

Besides, your kids already love you, even if they won't admit it. That should be enough for now. There's plenty of time to become BFFs with your offspring after they hit middle-age. Then you can *all* complain about "kids these days!"

And at least, by then, hopefully *they* can afford to pick up the check.

# On Cancel Culture

Maybe it's because I'm gay. As a gay man, I exist in a culture that, from a historical standpoint, is only just now emerging from an eternity of being "cancelled" by mainstream society, particularly by threatened "Christians" and conservatives.

Perhaps that's why I view the Right's latest brouhaha against "cancel culture" with unbridled delight. Their insistence that the Left "invented" cancel culture is downright hilarious, completely ludicrous, and loaded with a shitload of irony.

Let's jump into our time machines and travel back to 1852, shall we?

Historians point to Harriet Beecher Stowe's *Uncle Tom's Cabin*, published that year, as the first banned book in the United States. Believing it to have a pro-abolitionist agenda, and because it aroused heated debates about slavery, the Confederacy barred it from bookstores.

The Confederacy. You remember them, don't you? They're that wannabe-nation with a pro-slavery agenda that caused an American Civil War – and whose disgraced flag is still so popular in parts of the Deep South (and with others who should know better).

A decade or so later, Congress passed a law that prohibited the mailing of "pornographic materials." Among items too sexy for U.S postal service were textbooks about anatomy and/or reproduction, *The Canterbury Tales*, and anything written by Oscar Wilde.

"Sure sounds like a *left-wing* conspiracy to me!" I typed sarcastically.

Unbelievably, "comstockery" (the act of banning books) continues to this very day. The American Library Association publishes an annual list of the year's ten most challenged books.

In 2019, eight out of the ten were challenged for LGBTQ content. What a shock.

Ninth was Margaret Atwood's *The Handmaid's Tale*, for obvious (chauvinistic) reasons.

And #10 on the list? A book series so evil, it contains "actual curses and spells." Most of you have heard of it.

That's right! Some conservatives actually believe reading the *Harry Potter* series leads to Satanism.[11]

But let's talk about "cancellation" on a far more personal and destructive level.

Even today, even right now, as you're reading this – some "Christian" parents are disowning their own children when they learn he or she is LGBTQ.

Worse, a few parental monsters will even throw a teenaged or even pre-teen kid out into the streets when they make that discovery. It's horrific, but it still happens.

To me, that's the *ultimate* in "cancel culture." Created by the Right.

---

[11] Apparently *writing* the books leads to bigotry, but that's a whole different discussion.

So bitch, please.

After the endless indignities of Trump (and Weinstein and Musk and Epstein and Spacey and Cosby and…), many liberals are merely – and finally – screaming "ENOUGH!" to toxic ways and customs of the past.

And if we're doing so a bit too shrilly, too earnestly, perhaps it's because we've put up with racism, and sexism, and homophobia, and inequality, and double standards, and systemic and institutionalized bullshit for as long as we can remember.

The problem isn't that we're finally using the Right's tactics against them. The problem is that it took us this long to do so.

# An Essential Film-Viewing Guide for Today's Young Gay Male

"How could he even *claim* to be gay if he's never seen *Serial Mom*?!"

My good friend Erik was aghast! His new co-worker, a lad in his early 20s, had confessed that he'd never heard of the John Waters camp classic starring Kathleen Turner.

At first, I shared Erik's shock. But then, after giving it some thought, I tried to talk Erik down from his rage.

"Cut the kid some slack," I advised. "After all, there's way more content to keep track of now than when we were his age!"[12]

It's true! Erik and I grew up in the days of three TV networks, Top 40 radio, and movie theatres running ads in newspapers. At that time, there was only about 50 years' worth of films and film history, and 25 years of TV, to absorb and retain.

It was before cable, and streaming, offered us hundreds of channels and literally tens of thousands of film and TV titles from which to choose at any moment. It was before narrowcasting replaced broadcasting. It was before DIY

---

[12] Need evidence? Over 170 – that's one-hundred-seventy – drama series alone were eligible for Emmy consideration in 2022.

stardom, web series, social media, and influencers blurred all the lines.

Back in those dark ages, despite the lack of endless sources of constant show-biz chatter that we have now, it was ironically so much *easier* to stay on top of pop culture – especially gay pop culture.

That's because any film with gay content, or with a gay sensibility, was so incredibly rare, we jumped on it, then immediately told all our queer friends!

So as a service to my younger gay male readers, here's a by-no-means-complete list of 20 seminal movies made before 2000[13] (in order of release date) that you absolutely must see before discussing your love of films with your gay elders – thereby reducing the risk of invoking their gay ire.

### 1. *Rope* (1948)

Alfred Hitchcock's "one take" thriller about two men committing the perfect murder of a classmate (inspired by infamous gay murderers Leopold and Loeb) is as close to a gay film as one could hope to make (or see) in the 1940s.

In fact, in Patrick Hamilton's play on which this film is based, the men are explicitly homosexual. But thanks to the strict rules of Hollywood's Hayes Code, all overt signs of homosexuality were excised, leaving only subtext.

But, man, what subtext!

After hiding the body, then preparing for a dinner party, Brandon and Philip (played by John Dall and Farley Granger)

---

[13] This is by no means a definitive list. But it's mine. Your top 20 might be totally different and still be 100% correct.

breathlessly discuss their murderous act almost as if they're recalling an intense session of lovemaking. With their faces just inches apart, they lovingly recall each step of their crime ("How did you feel...?"), talking in increasingly hushed, heated, excited voices ("... And then?"), until the conversation comes to a quivering climax ("Exhilarated! ... How did you feel?"). It makes murder feel downright orgasmic!

In fact, there are so many shots of the two men standing close enough to kiss, you'd have to be Helen Keller to *not* see the homoeroticism.

As Brandon and Philip entertain their guests – with their dead classmate's body stashed in the chest on which they've served dinner – it feels as if more than one secret is hiding in plain sight.

God knows, Hitchcock was certainly no stranger to kink. One wonders, how much of the "joke" was Hitch in on? And how much was driven by Dall and Granger – both of whom, we've since learned, were gay themselves?

### 2. *All About Eve* (1950)

There are no out gay characters in this cautionary tale of life in the theatre (though venomous critic Addison DeWitt, played by George Sanders, is without a doubt a closeted queen), and there are no overt gay references. So why is this classic film beloved by gay men of all ages?

That's easy. Bette Davis' stage star Margo Channing is a female drag queen, swooping around in fabulous frocks, smoking furiously, throwing shade, getting drunk, pouting, and tossing fur coats like they were ponchos.

There are also glamorous people in gorgeous clothes, all living in fabulous apartments, dropping vicious, quotable one-liners. Oh, and if that wasn't already more than enough, there's also an early career appearance by Marilyn Monroe!

It all adds up to one fabulous movie. As backstabbing Eve Harrington, Anne Baxter is perhaps the film's one weak link – but somehow, her breathy, one-note performance only makes her Eve seem even *less* human, *less* sincere, and that much *more* monstrous!

As we watch, many of us fancy ourselves to be Margo Channing. Alas, in reality, most of us are probably more Birdie Coogan, the smart-assed personal assistant played by the always hilarious Thelma Ritter.

### 3. *Victim* (1961)

This story of a married lawyer who's blackmailed for being gay was incredibly frank for its time. Even more amazing? It starred a bona fide British film star and matinee idol, handsome Dirk Bogarde. You have to hand it to those Brits!

We like attorney Melville because he is not stereotypical, nor pathetic, nor suicidal. Straight audiences can accept him because he doesn't actually have sex with another man in the film. "I stopped seeing him because I WANTED HIM! Do you understand? I WANTED HIM!!" he finally exclaims to his wife after she asks, "Were you the other man?"

Sadly, there are limits, even in this film. When his wife asks if Melville loved the guy, he replies that "those feelings" can't be love. Now, that may be true for this character at that point in his life, but it's not a great message to send to gay audiences desperately starved for representation. But we took whatever we could get in those days.

### 4. *Valley of the Dolls* (1967)

A wildly unrealistic tale of three women who join show business, get addicted to drugs and booze, and meet their respective ruins. Total camp and a complete train wreck, this film adaptation of Jacqueline Susann's lurid bestseller is one of the first mainstream films to casually mention homosexuality without being *about* homosexuality – perhaps that's why gay men love it so. Or maybe it's because Patty Duke is supposed to be gay icon Judy Garland or because Sharon Tate is supposed to be gay icon Marilyn Monroe. Or maybe because the film is supposed to be a drama (seriously!) but is filled with unintentionally hilarious dialogue,[14] one-note performances, and the absurd notion that being married to Neely O'Hara makes for very effective gay-conversion therapy. Bonus points for Ms. Tate's delivery of "You know how bitchy fags can be!" – her line reading almost makes it sound like a compliment!

### 5. *The Boys in the Band* (1970)

Take a Valium (or two), light a joint, and throw back a Scotch (or three), before you settle in for the brutal original film adaptation of Mart Crowley's stage hit about nine gay friends (who don't actually like each other very much) gathering for a birthday party. Perhaps the first American film

---

[14] "Tony? Tony! Tony?! *Tony!!*" "Boobies! Boobies! *Boobies!*" "GOD?!"

to attempt an unflinching look at gay life, it's not fun, nor particularly funny – but remains a gritty, revealing window into that period of time when many gays were stuck somewhere between self-loathing and self-acceptance. You'll never appreciate more how far we've come than after seeing this time capsule

### 6. *Death In Venice* (1971)

If you still have a Valium left after watching *The Boys in the Band*, or if you haven't finished off that bottle of Scotch …

On its surface, this film does feel a little bit cringe-worthy by today's standards. But it's about so much more.

Our friend Dirk Bogarde is back, this time in a film version of Thomas Mann's classic 1912 novel, directed by Luchino Visconti.

Bogarde plays sickly composer Gustav von Aschenbach, who travels to a grand resort in Venice to rest and recover from heart disease, exhaustion and ennui.

Then Gustav spies Tadzio (Bjorn Andresen), the angelic adolescent son of fellow spa guests. Gustav becomes intrigued and reenergized by, and then completely obsessed with, the beautiful young blond. The composer begins to subtly stalk his new young muse throughout Venice.

So enamored of his new obsession, Gustav doesn't notice that the city is gripped by a cholera epidemic and is being constantly hosed down with disinfectant wash. Death is all around, but Gustav visits a barber, where he dyes his gray hair black to appear younger, and continues stalking, coming closer and closer and closer …

You're thinking "Ewwwww!" right about now, correct? But Gustav's not a pedophile. His pinning for the young lad isn't based on lust – or, at least, not *merely* on lust. Rather, it's the ideal of longing, lost innocence, lost youth and beauty, lost good health. Indeed, Tadzio represents life itself, whereas Gustav and Venice are both dying and rotting with decay.

Like young Tadzio, the film itself is painfully beautiful.

### 7. *Female Trouble* (1974)

Most people say *Pink Flamingos* is the "must-see" flick from Water's earlier career. But since I'm not a fan of swallowing my own vomit or watching singing assholes in extreme close up, I much prefer this follow-up!

This one also stars Waters' favorite "leading lady," 300-pound "male actress" Divine, as Dawn Davenport, a "hair-hopping" juvenile delinquent who runs away from home after her parents fail to give her a pair of "cha-cha heels" for Christmas. She's immediately raped by a bum (also played by Divine, out of drag), then gives birth to an ungrateful brat played by Mink Stole.

Dawn is taken in by a pair of felonious beauticians who encourage her to dedicate herself to a life of bizarre, violent crimes – culminating in a nightclub act wherein Dawn bounces on a trampoline (!) while shooting members of the audience dead.

She is arrested and quickly convicted. And once Dawn is finally strapped into the electric chair, she couldn't be happier – she sees this as the equivalent of an Academy Award for a life of crime!

There are lots of hilarious, quotable lines in this one, including my personal favorite, when Mink Stole informs her mom's boyfriend, "I wouldn't suck your cock if I were suffocating and there was oxygen in your balls!"

### 8. *Rocky Horror Picture Show* (1975)

This film adaptation of the British rock-and-roll stage musical, itself a spoof of 1950s horror films, was a rite of passage for many queer folk my age. While it may seem tame by today's sensibilities, it felt truly revolutionary back in the day.

Square school sweethearts Brad and Janet are driving one late, rainy night when their car has a blow-out. They seek help from the "castle down the road." They soon find themselves at a convention of motorcycle-riding space aliens, who have gathered to watch mad transvestite Dr. Frank-N-Furter (Tim Curry in a star-making turn) create a muscular sexual plaything in a gold Speedo named Rocky.

There's more bed-hopping than a season of *Dynasty*: after sleeping with his blond creation, Frank-N-Furter then seduces Janet, and then Brad. Janet then beds Rocky, and ... you get the idea! It's all set to a rollicking rock-and-roll score and ends with a big production number complete with – a swimming pool? – and the inspiring message "Don't dream it. Be it."

Home viewings of this one do not count. You've not really experienced *RHPS* until you've caught a midnight screening with cosplayers acting out in front of the screen and an audience screaming, throwing toast, tossing toilet paper, and all the rest of it. Good luck finding one – the NuArt in West

Los Angeles still screens it at midnight on Saturdays, but there aren't many others left!

### 9. *The Naked Civil Servant* (1975)

I take it as a personal affront whenever a young gay man asks me, "Who's Quentin Crisp?" Not just because I've played the iconic British gay legend (twice), but because he's truly one of our first champions and philosophers – daring to be openly and outrageously gay in a time and place where doing so got you beat up (repeatedly) and/or arrested.

In fact, Mr. Crisp was perhaps our first gender-fluid public personality – if that term had existed back in the early 1900s – daring to wear nail polish, frilly frocks, and "make-up at a time when even on women eye shadow was sinful!"

Faithfully based on Crisp's memoir, this British TV movie stars John Hurt as young Crisp, who's shunned by more "manly" gay men for being a sissy. But Crisp refuses to conform and conducts his life exactly as he wants – he lives alone and likes it, cultivating an eclectic group of friends and admirers, while struggling to find work without compromising his identity.

The highlight of the film comes when Crisp is wrongly arrested for soliciting for sex. He defends himself in court, declares himself as openly homosexual "for the world to see" on the witness stand – and is found innocent!

The film – packed with Crisp's philosophical quotes and witticisms – eventually played on PBS in America, turning Crisp into an international celebrity and a gay icon. (And rightly so, I might add!)

### 10. *The Ritz* (1976)

For the first time on screen, chubby chasing was not only referenced, but was a main plot point of a story! An overweight mafioso, running from hit men intent on killing him, hides out in a gay bathhouse – and then has to hide from a gay chubby chaser determined to bed him! Based on the hit Broadway farce, this film seems a bit ahead of its time, with its "no big deal" approach to the bathhouse milieu. In fact, back when I was in high school, I remember seeing this on the "CBS Late Movie," without so much as a viewer's advisory disclaimer. Perhaps it's because the cast – particularly Rita Moreno as bathhouse entertainer Googie Gomez and Treat Williams as a macho but high-pitched detective – is so fucking funny that you cannot possibly be offended.

### 11. *Taxi Zum Klo* (1980)

There was no way this film would ever play in Indiana theatres when I was in high school, but I read about it in *American Film* magazine. In fact, just reading about this film scared me more than a bit. It's all about a school teacher in a committed relationship with another man who still seeks anonymous (explicit!) sex with strangers. Some viewers argued then that he was a sex addict; others claimed it was an honest, unflinching look at gay life. I wasn't ready to watch this one until years after I'd moved to San Francisco, after I'd evolved into a more tolerant, modern-day homo. This is one of those films you *need* to watch, even though you might not necessarily enjoy watching it. If nothing else, it's a very good litmus test of where you are and what you want from your relationship(s).

## 12. *Cruising* (1980)

This movie, also a bit scary in its time, is now quite laughable in retrospect – once you get past some pretty disturbing violence, that is.

Forty years after its release, this movie is rightly remembered more for the uproar it created than for the actual film itself. The nascent "gay liberation" movement was rightly concerned the movie would label gay men in general, or leather queens specifically, as homicidal maniacs. They feared it would lead to increased violence against the LGBTQ community. They protested long and loud but were ultimately unsuccessful in stopping the film's production and release.

And that's too bad. Not because the film is offensive, but because it just plain sucks.

It's merely a flaccid cop thriller, all about a uniform beat cop recruited to go undercover and "play gay" to catch a serial killer preying upon patrons of Manhattan's leather-bar scene.

Sadly, the film skimps on relatable characters or believable plot points in favor of extended shots of Al Pacino furiously puffing poppers and dancing like an embarrassingly manic madman on the dance floor.

The end of the film *wants* you to wonder: Did the investigation turn Pacino's cop gay? Or was he gay but closeted all along?

But all you're likely to ponder is, why should anybody care?

Hardly a glowing recommendation, to be sure. But this film, like *Taxi Zum Klo*, should still be endured, at least once, for historical perspective.

### 13. *Mommie Dearest* (1981)

What? You haven't seen this one? Put this book down immediately, go watch this film, then report back.

Done? Congratulations! You are now officially a member of the "rest of us."

Why is this Joan Crawford biopic/Faye Dunaway kabuki vehicle such a gay classic?

Perhaps for the same reason Erik and I got into a heated argument on the bus home immediately after we saw a matinee.

He insisted then that Dunaway's performance deserved an Oscar nomination, if not the Academy Award itself!

"Ha!" I laughed in his face. Yes, I agreed, "Dunaway was certainly … committed!" But even if her over-the-top histrionics didn't turn off critics and the Academy, I argued, the film's high-gloss-yet-low-depth shallowness ensured it could never be taken seriously.

We were both right, as it turns out, and that's why I think this film has endured with gay audiences for over forty years. Dunaway is magnificent *and* horrific. The film is hilarious *and* gut-wrenching, beautifully shot but horribly directed. You feel for the characters as you laugh in their faces. A gorgeous, glamorous, fashion-filled shit show stuffed to overflowing with ugliness and hideosity.

Most gay men of my generation grew up living in conflicting "realities" simultaneously and appreciating the absurdity of it all, so maybe that's why *Mommie Dearest* struck such a chord with so many of us!

## 14. *Making Love* (1982)

Neither an honest nor important gay film, this was Hollywood's version of an "Honest, Important Gay Film." And in 1982, how could that not fail?

There are still a few things to admire about this low-budget story of a closeted, married doctor who finally admits his desire for other men in general, and for Harry Hamlin in particular. But overall, this film is more about how Hollywood saw us and less about who we really were. You can almost hear the film creak under the strain, as it attempts to be frank while also pulling its punches in an effort to be mainstream.

Kate Jackson of *Charlie's Angels* is pretty good as the unsuspecting network-executive wife. (In one scene, when she dismisses a TV script called "Hallinan's Dolls," you can't help but wonder if it's a dig at the series she'd left in disgust.)

Watching this one in an Indiana cinema half-filled with straight folk felt a bit like a radical, death-defying feat. When the two male leads kissed for the first time, then tumbled into bed and made out, I thought the roof of the theatre would blow off. My gay friend and I rushed out before the credits even began to roll.

## 15. *Victor/Victoria* (1982)

Although it was released the same year as *Making Love*, *Victor/Victoria* is adored as much as the other film is abhorred. Maybe it's because this one didn't force straight audiences to endure a man-on-man kiss. But other than that, it's pretty queer for a mainstream Hollywood release!

Julie Andrews is a down-on-her-luck singer in 1930s Paris who finds fame and riches when her gay friend convinces her to pose as a male drag queen. All is great, until she falls in love with confused straight gangster James Garner.

Alas, this film does cop out at a pivotal moment – letting Garner off the hook by allowing him to uncover Victor's secret *before* he kisses him/her (an error that was corrected in the Broadway re-do 15 years later). But overall, you will laugh heartily. You'll also admire this film for its guts – but don't confuse it with *Tootsie*, which is a fun feminist tale, not a queer one.

### 16. *My Beautiful Laundrette* (1985)

This one felt revolutionary in its day, for it was one of the first feature films in which lead characters were coincidentally gay. That is, their orientation and romance had absolutely nothing to do with the main story. Once again, British cinema was ready to "go there" when Hollywood wasn't. Daniel Day-Lewis first found fame as street thug Johnny, who abandons his gangster life to open a ritzy laundromat with his Pakistani boyfriend Omar (Gordon Warnecke) in working-class London. As the film ends, you'll feel as though you've witnessed diverse worlds you don't see in American films, because you have. You'll also feel hopelessly (and hopefully) romantic.

### 17. *Parting Glances* (1986)

It's 24 hours in the life of frustrated Manhattan writer Michael (Richard Ganoung), his stuffy live-in lover Robert (John Bolger), and his punk-rocker ex-boyfriend Nick (Steve Buscemi in his screen debut).

It's a bittersweet time for Michael. Robert is flying out in the morning for an extended work assignment in Africa. And

Nick, whom Michael has never truly gotten over, is battling AIDS. But there's no time for Michael to feel maudlin. He's too busy proofreading a rich friend's sci-fi gay-porn novel, playing nursemaid to Nick, then enduring an evening of bon-voyage dinners and parties for Robert.

Writer/director Bill Sherwood's first (and, sadly, his only) film is one of the first to tackle AIDS onscreen. It bursts with vibrant, true-to-life performances and circumstances, and captures a particular time and place – mid-1980s New York City and its queer-arts scene – with such micro-surgical precision that it feels like a literal time capsule of that period.

You'll laugh, you'll cry, and when it ends, you'll wish you could spend another 24 hours with Michael and his fascinating group of friends, lovers, exes, and co-workers.

### 18. *Maurice* (1987)

E.M. Forster's novel of frustrated first love gets the lush Merchant/Ivory treatment in this subtle, slow-moving, and completely swoon-worthy film adaptation.

Maurice and Clive (James Wilby, Hugh Grant) are Cambridge schoolmates who fall helplessly in love. But given that it's 1909, Clive eventually chickens out and marries Anne. There are lots of longing and loving glances between the two, and lots of bulky-knit sweaters, as Maurice continues to moon away for his caddish crush. That is, until Maurice meets Clive's swarthy gamekeeper Alec (Rupert Graves) – seeing them together suddenly gives Clive second thoughts about his life as a straight man.

Foppish Hugh Grant, or earthy Rupert Graves? Whom would *you* choose?

## 19. *Serial Mom* (1994)

"Is this the cocksucker residence?"

By far John Waters' best film (and Mr. Waters agrees), this hilarious spoof of true-life crime sagas tells the tale of suburban Baltimore housewife and mother Beverly Sutphin (Kathleen Turner), who flies into a murderous rage whenever someone insults her children (Ricki Lake and Matthew Lillard), steals her parking space (watch out, Mink Stole!), or wears white shoes after Labor Day (rest in peace, Patty Hearst!). Her weapons of choice include an air conditioner, a pay-phone receiver, and even a leg of lamb.

Once arrested, Beverly becomes a media sensation, leading her son's horror film-loving girlfriend to exclaim, "You're bigger than Freddie and Jason, only better. You're a real person!"

Although it pre-dates O.J. Simpson's murder trial, Waters later correctly pointed out that his film eerily predicted how *that* case would play out: a defendant doesn't have to be innocent to win, he or she simply has to discredit and humiliate every witness for the prosecution!

And don't worry. As a disclaimer explains, "no one involved in the crimes received any kind of financial compensation" for the film version of this "true story."

## 20. *First Wives Club* (1996)

A gay film? Not really. Like *All About Eve*, it's more about the film's bitchy gay sensibilities and quotable dialogue. Plus, this over-the-top comedy stars three of gaydom's favorite divas (Bette Midler, Goldie Hawn, and Diane Keaton) – or four, if you include an over-too-soon cameo by Stockard Channing that sets the plot in motion. Or five, if you count Maggie Smith as a hilarious matron of New York society. Or even six, because there's also a pre-*Sex and the City* Sarah Jessica Parker as a greedy gold-digging tramp. It's all about a trio of middle-aged women who seek revenge after being dumped for younger dames by their no-good ex-husbands. Hawn's youth-obsessed, alcohol-addled star "Eloise Elliot," in particular, is a character to whom many gay men "of a certain age" can certainly relate!

And here's one extra title:

### *The Celluloid Closet* (1995)

Watch this documentary to learn more about these and many more gay films (and to see the *real* Quentin Crisp), then read Vito Russo's exhaustive, page-turning textbook on which it's based to learn even more about queer-cinema history.

Other than *Celluloid Closet*, I wouldn't even attempt a list of important gay documentaries – of which there are many – because, for one thing, I'm not in that business!

But I've given you plenty of titles to start with. Since DVDs are a thing of the past, and since I'm old, it's up to *you* to hunt these gems down.

And once you've watched these titles, move onto these honorable mentions from the previous century (in no particular order): *Cabaret, Longtime Companion, Jeffrey, Death Becomes Her, Trick, Another Country, Different from the Others, Broken Hearts Club, The Sum of Us, Wilde, Beautiful Thing, Gods & Monsters, Capote, Torch Song Trilogy, Suddenly Last Summer* …

You're welcome.

# From Black to Worse

What the hell is happening to us?

This isn't your usual generic, geriatric "Those darned whippersnappers and their new-fangled music!" type of rant.

I'm not complaining about trends in music, television, or fashion. I'm not even bitching about the evolution of the English language.

I'm talking about the frayed, thread-bare fabric of American society today.

*What the hell is happening to us?*

It seems the very foundation of society is not only cracking but crumbling. At record speed. In front of our very eyes.

The rule of law has lost its teeth. Republicans ignore Congressional subpoenas and are almost never punished. A deranged throng invades the Capitol, foolishly believing they will somehow thwart democracy. Then the idiots express shock – *shock!* – when their criminal behavior results in criminal penalties.

A boy grabs his semi-automatic rifle, travels across state lines to go people hunting, murders two innocents, then not only walks away scot-free, but becomes a poster boy to racists and needle-dicks everywhere.

Science is ignored. Higher education is ridiculed.

Social media is turning us against each other, but most folks can't bear the thought of logging off.

Automobile fatalities are off the charts as drivers become increasingly reckless, causing more frequent and deadlier accidents than ever before.

Hell, even simple self-preservation, once the most basic fundamental of life, seems beyond some of us. Our lakes and rivers are drying up, our oceans are rising, our forests are in flames, and the ice caps are melting. Global warming and climate change are now simply undeniable as photos of dried lakebeds and exposed sunken boats have become commonplace. Yet so many (citizens *and* corporations) ignore the blatant evidence and continue to lie and deny.

*What the hell is happening to us?*

Why have so many Americans become hateful, vengeful, and so God-damned stupid?

I have a theory. And it may shock you.

I blame Barack Obama.

It's not *directly* his fault. Rather, it's the result of his presidency. Or rather, the *reaction* to his presidency.

I grew up in 1960s/1970s Indiana. So I know all about the "closet racist." Hell, I was surrounded by them. Chances are, so were you! You know the type…

He said things like, "She's pretty for a Black girl." Or, "He's Black, but he's just like us." Or, "After five minutes, you'll forget he's Black." And he actually thinks he's giving a compliment!

She's never joined the Klan. She's never used the "n-word," at least not outside her home. She knew to keep her prejudices to herself, especially as the new century began.

In my hometown of Kokomo, they jokingly referred to Apperson Way, the main street through the town's "Black neighborhood," as "African Way." All in good, clean fun.

Except to me. That's when I first started speaking out. Back then, the conversation usually went something like this:

"That's racist!" said I.

"Lighten up!" say they.

"It's not funny!"

"You have no sense of humor!"

"Calling it 'African Way' is offensive!"

"Well, they *came* from Africa, didn't they?"

"We *brought them here against their will!*"

At which point, having lost patience with precocious little Leon, the closet racist would chuckle, tousle my hair, and turn their attention back to the other grown-ups.

But would they ever consider themselves actual racists? *Never!*

If a Black man were promoted over him to become his boss, he would be angry. *But he's not racist!*

Or if a Black family moved in next door, she'd consider moving her family to another part of the suburbs. *But she's not racist!*

They were 100% okay with Black people – so long as they knew "their place."

So imagine their pain, their shock, their confusion and angst, when a Black man won the highest office of the land and became the "boss" of us all. It angered them. It made them just a little bit nuts.

Now multiply that man and woman by, say, 10 or 12 million or more.

*That's* what the hell has happened to us.

The idea that a Black man could become the leader of the free world was incomprehensible to these closet cases. Obama's victory pushed many of these folks out of their racist closets. They had to do *something*!

After all, the non-closeted racists had wasted no time. Vile posts and graphics online were instant and inescapable. We had to endure the ridiculous, reactionary "Tea Party." We had to listen while they blamed Obama for every upset and disappointment in their lives.

But even to the still-timid closet racists, *everything* was the Black guy's fault – even though they still knew, in their dark little hearts, that saying *why* they truly felt way this was still completely unacceptable.

They made shit up. Crazy shit, like "He's a Muslim!" and "He's coming for your guns!" and "He's a foreigner!" and "He's about to impose martial law!" and "Obamacare means death panels will decide who lives or dies![15]"

They railed against his tan suit. They railed against his wife's bare arms. All while ignoring his many real accomplishments.

But they still would *never* call themselves racists! Even though they knew they were.

That cognitive dissonance began to drive them bonkers.

---

[15] The fact that insurance companies basically already perform this service was lost on them.

Speaking of bonkers, tangerine-colored Donald Trump, a known racist since the 1980s, took up the anti-birther campaign, demanding to see Obama's birth certificate.

And when that 300-pound malignant fistula glided down his gilded escalator in 2015, spewing bigoted bullshit as he announced his candidacy for President, the once-closeted racists found their poster boy. Trump wasn't afraid to spout racist bile. He was speaking their language. He was voicing their rage.

And boy, were they enraged! After eight years of that Black bastard, they were pissed. They were exhausted. And now, they had a guy who wouldn't judge them for being racist. Because he was a big one, too.

Once elected (and not by winning the popular vote), Trump emboldened these burgeoning bigots further.

Hearing a President of the United States of America respond to the blatant 2017 hate crime in Charlottesville with the words "there are good people on both sides" gave them full permission to finally act out on their worst instincts. Listening to the asshole refer to African and Latin nations as "shithole countries" empowered them. Emboldened them.

"How can it be *wrong* if the *President* says it?"

"If *he* can spew racist bullshit, then *we* can, too!"

And that permission for crass behavior has since spilled over into the rest of American life. If the man holding the most respected office in the land demonstrates nothing but disrespect for all things good and decent, well, then you're a fool if *you* follow the rules now.

It's why highway fatalities have skyrocketed. Why crime is exploding. It's why too many people basically volunteered to die of COVID, all in the name of "owning those libs!" It's why common sense and common courtesy are both thin on the ground.

It's why people (who should have better things to do) are up in arms over a Black Little Mermaid.

That's how we ended up with a nation full of "Karens" (of *all* genders), ready to act out at a moment's notice should reality present obstacles to their perceived (white) privilege.

Will pointing fingers and laying blame change anything or make matters worse? I don't have an answer to that question. But I *do* know, if we hope to ever bring civility back into our national discourse, we *must* shine a spotlight on these assholes each and every time they act out.

That's why, just like when I was younger, I try to call out bigotry whenever I see or hear it, be it on social media, or in "real life." We must *never* tolerate it, nor accept it as "normal." Because it is *not* normal. It should not be tolerated, no matter how accustomed and immune to it we become.

We will never abolish racism. But we *must* make racists ashamed of themselves again. We must constantly and consistently remind them that their behavior is absolutely, positively, *unacceptable* by *any* standard. We must shut down any hint of prejudicial language or behavior with zero tolerance.

When it's safe to do so, risk making a scene when you witness racism.

Cut no slack. Show no quarter.

We need to shame these hateful racists.

We must shoo them back into their closets where they belong.

It's a start…

# Fuck Facebook

Facebook knows what pisses you off. It has from the beginning.

And it's making a fortune keeping you constantly outraged.

If you haven't been living under a rock, you've probably heard about Frances Haugen, the former Facebook employee who testified to Congress in 2021 (and "brought receipts" via screen captures she smuggled out of Facebook headquarters) about how the platform's algorithm is designed to keep users seeing posts that anger them.

And that's just the tip of the iceberg.

News outlets shared the many documents she provided, dubbed the "Facebook Papers," which detailed some extremely serious lapses in morality and judgment at the social-media giant – how it benefitted January 6 insurrectionists, how it aided in actual genocide of Muslims in Myanmar beginning in 2016, how it continues to contribute to human trafficking, and how it consistently puts profits above common sense and human decency.

The list goes on. And on. And on.

Let's talk about Facebook's love of "click bait" and why it needs to keep you in a constant state of anger and fear. For starters, take this revelation about an internal experiment by a researcher at the platform's headquarters:

The researcher created a profile for fictional "Carol Smith" of Wilmington, North Carolina. The researcher entered that "Carol" was interested in politics, Christianity, and parenting, and signed "Carol" up as a fan of Trump and Fox News. The researcher then sat back and watched as, within two days, Facebook's algorithm suggested to "Carol" that she join groups and sites devoted to QAnon.

Within a week, her newsfeed was filled with conspiracy theorists and groups that violated Facebook's own rules on hate speech.

Poor "Carol" never asked for any of it!

Why?

Because Mark Zuckerberg & Co. know folks are much more likely to click, share, and comment on posts that infuriate. Posts that make people feel all warm and fuzzy inside get far less traction and engagement.

And engagement equals profit.

They also have enough data on their users to predict how each of us define "bad news." If you're a democracy-loving Democrat, you see a lot of news about Trump and his loony band of misfits on your newsfeed. (Trust me.) Conversely, I assume, if you're a white supremist, you can expect to see a bunch of posts about Black Lives Matter.

Many content providers, including politicians and news organizations, see that Facebook favors "bad news" – so that's what they keep posting. Because the whole point is engagement. They know if they post "happy" content, people won't see it, and thus, won't interact.

In fact, according to Haugen's testimony, many international leaders have reached out to Facebook to complain that, because of this algorithm, they must make more and more alarmist and confrontational statements if they hope to be seen, and/or to generate interaction from users (and voters).

Facebook literally sows the seeds of dissention for profit.

Let me repeat that:

*Facebook literally sows the seeds of dissention for profit.*

Yet its public mission statement is "bringing the world closer together." What a load of horseshit.

In my 2020 book *SUB-LEBRITY,* I mused that the ensuing social-media outrage from Donald Trump's campaign (and later, presidency) killed *Old Dogs & New Tricks*.

When we launched the show in 2011, attracting and interacting with viewers and fans on Facebook was a breeze. Our posts got tons of engagement in those early days.[16]

Slowly, that began to change.

My posts about *ODNT* got less engagement. Meanwhile, my posts raging about Trump, my public smackdown of "Cindy Brady," *et al.*, always generated enormous feedback. In fact, the resulting media firestorm from the "Brady Debacle"[17] brought me more media attention (and more new followers) within one week than my peaceable, award-winning series did over five years!

---

[16] It was also before Facebook began limiting how many people see non-promoted posts – in hopes users would pay for exposure.

[17] Just Google my name if you're unfamiliar with the "Brady Debacle" – or better yet, buy *SUB-LEBRITY* wherein I regurgitate the story one last time.

I eventually realized it was now impossible to break through all the online anger to raise money for, and to promote, our show – even if I didn't have hard evidence.

Well, I have it now. And I was wrong.

Trump didn't kill the show.

Facebook did.

Trump merely knew how to leverage Facebook to his full advantage, and how to make it all about him. Fucking narcissist.

So the world's most popular social media site is intentionally and literally turning us against one another. Where does that leave us?

Most users aren't ready to disconnect, at least not completely. I, for one, have used Facebook as a virtual scrapbook for over a decade.

All the same, I've recently downloaded all of my photos and videos from Facebook, just in case. (It's time-consuming, but otherwise easy.) Because if Facebook allows Trump to further tear our country apart with more lies and hate, I will delete my account in a New York second.

Meanwhile, there's something we *can* do while still on the platform:

We can stop using Facebook to voice anger, to argue with others, to boast of our moral superiority.

I know, I know. If you follow me on Facebook, you're rolling your eyes right now, because you know I'm always rushing in where angels fear to tread (yes, making me a fool!).

That's because I was bullied as a young kid, so insults don't penetrate. I've been able to fling myself into the muck with little concern for my feelings. I just kept hurling insults back tenfold. But what does it accomplish, other than perpetuating Zuckerberg's pathetic profiteering, and keeping my feed full of infuriating bullshit?

Despite my once-constant political posts, I frankly doubt I've changed one person's mind. I've merely strengthened the political and ideological bubbles Facebook keeps us in. Posting insults and links on "how to leave a cult" on Marjorie Taylor Greene's and Lauren Boebert's profile pages – and engaging in the resulting "arguments" – may have made me feel good (or even superior) in the immediate instant. It even felt a little fun, in a sick and twisted way – at first, anyway.

But that elation is short-lived once you realize you're screaming into a vacuum and that your wit isn't enough to change *anyone's* point of view. People either agree with you or they hate you.

The corrosive effect of being able to tell people off – even people who have rightfully earned our scorn – becomes toxic to everyone. The old saying really is true. "Holding onto anger is like drinking poison and expecting the other person to die."

Let's be honest. Merely bitching on Facebook alone doesn't make any of us an "activist" (despite what some of my show-biz colleagues claim). In fact, the term "hashtag activist" was coined around the time of Occupy Wall Street to refer to folks who talk a good game online, but who otherwise sit out protests, don't call their reps, or (God forbid) don't even vote!

So let's promote what we love, instead of bashing what we hate – like how Maya Angelo recommended attending peace rallies but avoiding anti-war protests. It's about keeping the message – and your mentality – positive!

Go to the pages of the politicians and activists you admire. Tell them how much you appreciate them! If you're able, ask how you can volunteer to help their cause.

If you absolutely *must* go to the pages of those leaders with whom you disagree, resist commenting with disgust to the lunatic ravings of their supporters. Instead, post comments that are argument-proof.

Share Bible verses that expose those leaders as hypocrites with no further comment.

Turn into a southern belle and kill them with kindness (*"Oh, bless your little heart"*).

Refuse to engage with any and all trolls who try to bait you.

Better yet, use your energy to report posts that promote violence or white supremacy.

I've done enough time in "Facebook Jail" to know that if enough people complain about a post or comment, Facebook will punish the person responsible – even if the post or comment doesn't technically break their nebulous, ever-changing (double) standards.

That's why crackpots still post nonsense about the pandemic or white supremacy, often without consequence, but anyone who calls them a "covid-iot" or a racist risks suspension.

I urge everyone to resist that urge to give in to venom.

Let's stop Zuckerberg from getting richer still from hate and division.

Let's stop arguing politics on Facebook.

Let's go back to posting positive stories, fun photos – you know, the content we used to share back when Facebook still felt fun!

Remember those days?

Perhaps fewer "Friends" will see your posts. But maybe – just maybe – if enough people say "enough!" we can cut into their profits and send a message at the same time.

In the meantime, contact your representatives *today* (via phone, email, and "snail mail") and urge them to investigate and regulate Facebook (and Twitter, too!).

Facebook is not invulnerable. Remember MySpace? Friendster?

There was a time when America Online fancied itself just as powerful as Facebook would become. TimeWarner (as it was then called) spent millions to merge with AOL and added them to their corporate name. For a while anyway.

Who uses AOL these days?

Who even *remembers* AOL these days?

# Where There's Smoke, There's Ire

I've been with my wonderful husband Laurence for over 30 years.

And I've been good friends with my very first boyfriend, Erik, for 40 years.

Yet my longest-lasting relationship isn't with a man. My most passionate, tortured, "on-again/off-again" love affair has been with a lady. Perhaps some of *you* have also been seduced by the evil bitch's lethal charms and false promises of tranquility.

I'm talking about Lady Nicotine.

Now, I don't believe in playing "blame the parents." But in this case, I was clearly genetically predisposed. Norm and Judy both smoked while I was growing up. In those days, Dad was rarely seen without a smoke. In fact, on horseback in his cowboy hat, flannel shirt, and a cigarette in hand, he was the spitting image of the Marlboro Man.

Mom was more discreet. But she loved tobacco just as much, smoking while pregnant with both my older sister Tammy and me. (No judgments, please. It was the early 1960s, before common sense and the Surgeon General's warnings really kicked in. Everyone smoked, everywhere. Mom is and always has been a wonderfully conscientious woman and mother.)

I wasn't always a full-blown nicotine addict. In fact, as a child, I was an extremely militant anti-smoker. In grade school, I terrorized my parents with photos of black lungs and discussions of the "artificial lung" a teacher used to demonstrate the immediate dangers of smoking. When I checked the mail, I put any and all solicitations from the American Cancer Society or the American Lung Society right on top.

For a while, I was truly terrified that Mom and Dad would drop dead of cancer at a moment's notice. But my non-stop harassment did not one bit of good. You truly can't make an addict change unless/until he/she/they is/are ready.

I was just as insufferable as an early adult. In fact, my first roommate smoked. So inside the decorative ashtray Mom had given me as my first housewarming gift, I placed a card. It read: "Not for Use as a Real Ashtray." Roommate Dee Dee knew I was deadly serious.

It all changed when I first saw the 1981 film *Only When I Laugh*. Actress Marsha Mason played a troubled, alcoholic, chain-smoking actress in this film version of her husband Neil Simon's "serious" play *The Gingerbread Lady*. Now, I fancied myself a tortured artist back in those days – or at least I aspired to be one. And boy, Ms. Mason made smoking look so fun, so fulfilling, so fucking *cool*.

Within two hours, the movie erased over 17 years of militancy. After the end credits, I left the theatre, went to a drug store, and bought my very first pack of cigarettes – for 63 cents!

I started with Carlton, the brand so low in tar and nicotine that they're practically almost good for you. In fact, writer Fran Lebowitz wrote that smoking a Carlton was less like smoking, and "more like inhaling deeply in a warm room."

Ah, Fran! Perhaps the only person who loves smoking more than I!

Once I was able to fully inhale, I switched to Marlboro Lights (although I think I must have tried almost every brand at least once before I turned 21). Soon, I was a full-blown, foul-smelling heavy smoker. And I absolutely loved it.

What happened to the Leon who *despised* smoking? Why did I fall so hard, after being so humorless and judgmental just a year previously? In those days, many actors smoked in their films without a content warning. I'd grown up worshipping all things Hollywood, so it was an easier shift that one might expect.

There was also a "daredevil" aspect to it that appealed to me, especially since I never got that kind of charge from playing sports. Yes, I'm comparing smoking cigarettes to playing sports. That Lady really can twist your logic.

Additionally, I was a bit of a spazz back then (still am, some say), and smoking gave me an excuse to stop, sit back, and do nothing but just *be* – at least for a couple of minutes at a time.

Smokers hadn't yet been relegated to sidewalks and alleyways, but being an open, unapologetic smoker in the early

1980s was still a bit punk, a sign of subtle rebellion. Smoking fit into the iconoclastic personality I was trying to adopt. I was just too cool to care when people complained – including co-workers, friends, and potential boyfriends.

When a disappointed date told me, "I just can't be with a smoker. The smell makes me go limp," I replied, "Your loss, dude." I wasn't about to give up on my "main squeeze" for a potential "side piece." Occasionally I tried to muster through an entire dinner-and-movie without indulging – but I don't think I ever made it.

Protestations, such as, "How can you smoke a stinky cigarette after such an incredible meal?" were usually answered with "Shut the fuck up," but said with a shit-eating smile, natch!

Eventually, I made a few half-hearted attempts to stop. I vividly remember the first time I tried to quit. After work, I sat in my dark apartment, watching videos, and tried, tried, *tried* not to think about smoking. But it was all I *could* think about. After about only an hour, I was rocking back and forth on my sofa like some deranged mental patient. About thirty minutes later, I was at the corner store, buying a pack and giving up on giving them up.

Those early attempts never stood a chance. As I stated earlier, addicts never change until they *want* to change. I knew it would behoove me to quit, but I never truly wanted to. So I never did. Eventually, I began a hot sexual affair with a guy who didn't say anything about my smoking, so I more or less gave up on dating for real … for a while.

By the early 1990s, smoking was considered only slightly less offensive than, oh, child molestation? And the addiction itself was only slightly more affordable than a cocaine habit.

But I *still* didn't quit.

When people complained about second-hand smoke, I reminded them I didn't drive a car[18] but they did (which creates more carcinogenic pollution than my mere ciggie), so again, words to the effect of *shut the fuck up*.

Then I met Laurence.

God love him, he didn't pressure me to quit although he often encouraged me to give it up. In fact, he was one of those annoying people who could smoke one or two cigs a day without developing a full-blown addiction.

Bastard.

I soon fell in love with the bastard. We moved in together. I dangled out of windows to smoke. I perched over the edge of balconies. He sometimes joined me. But he never stopped his casual campaign for me to give them up.

Laurence's subtle nudges were far more effective than the constant incessant hounding of others. As much as I loved to smoke, I realized how much easier life would be if I didn't. I wouldn't have to pop breath mints constantly. *Or* spend a fortune at the dry cleaners. *Or* wash my hair twice a day.

Then there was the expense. A pack no longer cost just 63 cents. Between inflation, price hikes, and ever-increasing state and federal taxes, cigarettes had more than tripled in price – and continued to climb. Consuming a pack a day was getting pricey. Now that I was a full-blown professional actor, I had

---

[18] I didn't drive for over a decade, an easy feat in San Francisco.

expenses like classes and headshots and union dues. Since I was also now in a serious relationship, I had to at least *consider* the desires of my partner.

By then, both my parents had kicked the habit. They encouraged me to join them in the smoke-free world. And I couldn't tell my parents to "Shut the fuck up."

*Okay. Let's get serious and give quitting another try!*

I gave up my beloved Marlboro Lights and switched to American Spirits. I figured, between the higher cost and the change of taste, I'd find it easier to give them up.

Ha! Within a week, I loved American Spirits, and realized that Marlboro Lights tasted like formaldehyde.[19]

When I discussed quitting with my doctor, he joked that nicotine was probably in my DNA by now. At least I *think* he was joking. He prescribed the anti-depressant Zyban, and I tried to quit for real.

I lasted until 3:30 p.m.

Soon, I tried again. I lasted half a day.

Then again. For a full day.

Then again. Three days.

And again. For about two weeks!

Eventually I endured *eight months* without lighting up. I was very proud of myself. So was Laurence.

At least he *was*. After a heated argument – *I no longer remember about what!* – I was so pissed off, I wanted to lash out. I rushed out, bought a pack, and smoked them furiously – destroying eight months' of self-discipline.

Boy, I really showed *him*, didn't I?

---

[19] Think I'm kidding? Google " Marlboro ingredients"!

If at first (or one-hundred-and-first) you don't succeed, try, try again!

Ironically, stress rarely brought me back to that wicked weed. In fact, during one particularly stressful week after moving to particularly stressful Los Angeles, my cat died, I was diagnosed with pre-melanoma skin cancer, and I wrecked my car. Yet through all of that, I was never tempted to take even a single puff.

It was usually *good* news that unraveled my ever-increasing willpower. As soon as I nailed a sought-after audition, or landed a part I really wanted, or got a mention in a really good review, I *had* to celebrate with my good old friend, that vexing vixen named Lady Nicotine.

But she and I were no longer hot and heavy lovers – more like exes who meet for occasional hook-ups.

Then I'd climb back on the wagon and manage to stay there for increasingly longer periods each time. I'd abstain for about six months, smoke for about six months. Rinse and repeat. And repeat. And repeat.

*Well, at least I've cut my smoking by half!* I rationalized after a few years.

As much as I worshipped Lady Nicotine, I had nothing on my older sister Tammy. She and the Lady first became acquainted in grade school and remained life-long buds.

I worshipped my older sister, whom I called "Sissy," in our earliest years. I followed her like a shadow; I even went with her on visits to the bathroom. I'd sit on the floor, and we'd just continue talking as though there was nothing at all peculiar about it! We played Barbies together. Watched scary movies together on late-night TV. Made up dance routines to some of Mom's old 45 records.

Tammy was what was called a "tomboy" in those days. She still liked girly clothes and make-up when the occasion called for it, but she also wouldn't hesitate to punch a kid if he said something nasty about her. Or about her baby brother.

*Me and my Sissy*

Once we were both in grade school, she became embarrassed by this delicate little sissy boy who was her brother – especially since I spent the first several days of first grade bursting into tears and wailing her name when I saw her in the lunch room.

"*Sissy!!* When are we going *home??*"

Like smoking and swearing, her hormones and blonde good looks also kicked in during grade school. Tammy didn't have much time or purpose for a clingy baby brother. By fourth grade, she'd already developed a reputation as a boy-crazy wild cat for making out with boys during recess. She also never hesitated to throw herself into a fight in the school yard, against girls *and* boys. If my parents had been millionaires, her behavior would've been described as "madcap."

I was more of a quiet book worm, and two and one-half years younger which, by the time we reached middle school, was a huge "generation gap." We no longer had anything to talk about. She got into big-hair rock music. I became obsessed with TV. We drifted apart – but she'd still "have my back" if "push came to shove" with bullying classmates.

One day, Mom found Tammy's hidden pack of Kool's. Mom sat Tammy down on the staircase of our house and forced her to smoke every cigarette left in the pack. Perhaps Mom thought Tammy would turn green, get sick, and swear off smoking for good. Not my big sister. Tammy sat there and smoked. And smoked. And smoked.

And she never, ever stopped.

By the time she was an adult, she easily smoked at least two packs a day. She'd joke she was born with a lit cigarette in her mouth (to which I'd always reply, "How painful for *Mom*!")

Whenever I flew home for a visit, Tammy and I bonded over many, many, many smokes – as well as other smoke-able weeds. Despite our many differences, our shared dark senses of humor always helped us find common ground.

I never once worried about her heavy smoking because she seemed indestructible by this point. She'd survived a number of serious car accidents, numerous spills off horses and motorbikes, four marriages to some real jerks, a stint behind bars for bounced checks, a few health scares, and more. She never met a recreational drug she didn't like, yet she remained tougher than old shoe leather. In many ways, I think Tammy was the *son* Dad always wanted.

Every so often, I'd see cracks in her tough exterior. Once, in the 1990s, she was shocked – *shocked!* – by Nine Inch Nails' song "Closer." She was aghast that her teenaged daughters were listening to lyrics like "I want to fuck you like an animal." I chuckled as I reminded her of how aghast Mom had been by some of the music Tammy listened to as a teen.

*Me and Tammy in 2010*

I should have seen it as a sign of things to come. Tammy's fourth marriage was to a conservative man who eventually became a MAGA maniac. Sadly, he seemed to change Tammy's once-liberal nature. I found talking with Tammy was now loaded with too many potential land mines. We went years without communicating.

But when "Cindy Brady" tried to sic her Trump-loving fans on me in 2016, Tammy sent Ms. Olsen a message, threatening to fly to California and personally "kick her ass" if she didn't "lay off my baby brother."

She still had my back, after all these years. Despite now being polar opposites, I couldn't swear her off for good. I loved her, and I know she loved me.

One day in late summer 2019, I got a text from my niece.
"Mom has lung cancer."
And just 41 days later, my indestructible big sister was dead.

I got to town mere hours before she died. My niece ushered me into Tammy's darkened, crowded hospice room. A TV mounted in the corner was displaying local news, but nobody was watching. Everyone's attention was focused on Tammy on the bed in the middle of the room, attached to all manner of beeping medicinal machines, being propped up by her husband, her daughters, and a nurse, as she desperately gasped for air. Her battle to breath was intense and unrelenting. Sometime later, as they lowered her back onto her bed, she glanced over and saw me sitting in a corner. She seemed surprised to see me. I waved at her. She lifted a finger, weakly wiggled it at me to wave "hello," then collapsed with exhaustion until the *next* battle to get air into her diseased lungs.

She lost the battle early the next morning.

It didn't seem possible. Tammy was always so invulnerable, so willing to jump into a fight to protect her family or its honor, with no fear or worry for her own safety. It was almost inconceivable that now, so suddenly, she was ... just ... *no more*. Who would be the scrappy protector of our family now?

I decided shortly thereafter I *must* escape Lady Nicotine's ruthless grip once and for all. Not because I feared Tammy's fate for myself – a statement that is evidence of my wildly dysfunctional relationship with smoking. I finally told Lady Nicotine to beat it because I don't want my parents to ever lose a child again.

My life goal became *Saving Private Leon*.[20]

A week or two after I'd returned to California, a Facebook friend (who claims to be a psychic) sent me a private message. She claimed she'd been visited by Tammy (whom she'd never met, nor had she met me) in a dream. Tammy told her that it was okay if Leon needed to smoke to get through this trying time. I wasn't sure I believed the psychic, but it *did* sound like something Tammy would tell me. Tammy *was* a bit devotional in her love of psychics. Then the psychic mentioned she was seeing leaping frogs – and I instantly flashed back to one of my favorite memories of my sister.

We were in our late 20s. I was back in Indiana for a summer visit. We had gotten wildly stoned and a little drunk with her current boyfriend, then we tried to quietly sneak back into our parents' house well past midnight. As we opened the sliding-glass door into the dining room, we saw Mom standing in the hallway, wide awake, arms folded, clearly annoyed. We instinctively, immediately tried to "play" sober. But just then, a gigantic frog – appearing from out of nowhere – jumped between Tammy's legs into the dining room! Tammy and I both screamed like Fay Wray, then burst into hysterical laughter as

---

[20] Just months later, COVID descended and intensified my goal!

we collapsed onto the floor trying to catch it – exposing us as obviously drunken stoners to our mother.

The story became family folklore over time. But the psychic could not have known! I hung up the phone and burst into tears.

I never invited Lady Nicotine to join my mourning, no matter how sad I became over losing my big "Sissy."

It's now over three years later, and I'm rather surprised by how successful I've been.

However, in the interest of full disclosure, there *have* been a handful of instances when I've allowed myself to indulge in a smoke – or a pack – during those years.

Once was when I was invited to submit a writer's "sample packet" to *The Late Show with Stephen Colbert*.

Like receiving good news, writing under deadline is still a huge trigger. So this was a double whammy! I had only a weekend to magically pull a monologue, a commercial parody, *and* a skit out of my ass and get them down on paper.

*Fuck it*, I decided, and allowed myself just one pack while I paced and spoke to myself (outside) trying out lines. I smoked as I sat in my car reading the show's very specific "style manual" for its scripts. Once I emailed in my submission, I celebrated with the last cig in the pack, then went back to being a reformed nicotine addict.[21]

That week in early November 2020, as we waited to learn the identity of our next President – Biden? Trump? – was also too stressful to resist the Lady's delusional promise of solace.

---

[21] I wasn't hired, but thanks for asking.

As we waited out the days for all votes to be counted, I succumbed. Laurence was less than pleased. But I promised to climb back on the wagon once a winner was declared – even if it was Trump – so he kept his mouth shut. And I kept my promise.

Perhaps it's all about one's mindset. Because when earlier attempts failed, it took me weeks or months – sometimes years – to work up the resolve to give it another shot. But now, when I've allowed myself to be a bad boy for a pack or two, I've been able to quit – *just stop!* – immediately after each lapse. I can walk away from the Lady without much stress or other signs of withdrawal. Like a reformed alcoholic, I will always refer to myself as a smoker, however, or as a recovering smoker. *Never* an "ex-smoker." I haven't *quit* smoking; I've *stopped* smoking. The urge never truly goes away for good. Every so often, after dinner, the craving still hits me like a punch to the stomach!

I just don't want to be an active smoker any longer.

An unexpected post-script:

While driving home after writing the first draft of this essay, I thought, *you are writing, and you're writing about smoking. Buy yourself a pack!*

I had no sooner lit up when I had a realization so definitive that I spoke it aloud to myself in the car.

"Leon, you just wrote maybe ten pages, including some very painful memories, without so much of a single puff. *You don't need cigarettes to write!*"

May that be the last time I use *that* excuse.

But I know better than to make promises I might not keep.

If I make it to 80, I might just invite Lady Nicotine back into my life.

Stay tuned.

# Secrets of a Successful Long-Term Relationship?

I never imagined I'd ever *not* be single, though I certainly fantasized about being one-half of a couple through most of my twenties.

Truth is, I didn't think I had the skill set for marriage.

Hell, I couldn't even keep a good romance going for more than a few weeks. I would either lose interest or do something weird that scared them off – like missing a lunch date by oversleeping after an all-night *Dynasty* marathon or jumping out of a potential boyfriend's bed at one a.m. because *"you snore and I need some sleep!"*

Sometimes I'd sink a potential romance by being far too honest far too early. (*"You asked me if I liked your new haircut! Do you want me to lie?"*) My overly opinionated nature sank more than one ship before it sailed. (*"You actually liked* Showgirls? *It's a rancid piece of shit!"*)

More than once, I'd change my mind in the middle of a date, deciding *not* to take it to the next level. I'd cut the evening short, and leave the other guy confused and pissed off.

For example, I once lost interest in a intimidatingly sexy guy after he confessed he went jogging every morning at 4:30 a.m. I couldn't imagine myself waking up that early for *any* reason, not even to smoke a cigarette, so I bid him adieu.

Off stage, my timing is bad, and I'm not great at picking up on cues. That jogger I ran away from? I excused myself as we were settling onto his living-room floor, following a romantic dinner. I realize now, 35 years later, that we would've made it to his bedroom if I *hadn't* left early. (And maybe, just maybe, I would've discovered he *was* worth waking up early for!)

I could also be incredibly picky. I broke off with one potential boyfriend because he wore nothing but t-shirts, cut-offs, tube socks, and gigantic tennis shoes. Every. Single. Day.

My general know-it-all nature certainly was a great safe-sex aid. It's little wonder how I survived the 1980s.

If a prospective beau was foolish enough to make a crack about my smoking, he got an immediate heave ho.

And if a guy told me he was Republican? I made like the Road Runner and left him in a cloud of dust.

During the few occasions I found myself in a relationship lasting beyond a few dates, I'd become restless and bored. It's not that I was looking to cheat. I was just far more interested in the pursuit than the acquisition.

Maybe I was guilty of that old Groucho Marx joke: "I don't want to belong to any club that would have me for a member."

I'm one lucky son of a bitch to have met Laurence over 30 years ago. He shares many of my obsessions, and even appreciates the obsessions that we don't share. He isn't threatened by my occasional self-destructive tendencies. He's able to laugh at most of my foibles and shortcomings, but is also quick to praise my talents, abilities and other attributes.

He has a great sense of humor and is endlessly hilarious. I marvel at his ability to keep me on track, financially, artistically, and personally. He has a near-photographic memory and an incredible facility with numbers, dates, and figures. For example, he can tell you exactly when an Olivia Newton-John single peaked, and where, on the Billboard charts 40 years ago.

I also greatly admire his talent at what he does (producing and managing high-end special events) and I'm grateful when he uses those skills to help produce my foolish little show-biz projects from time to time. He keeps me current with my SAG dues and makes sure I never miss a deadline. He gives me advice on how to handle difficult directors, cranky co-stars, and the occasional overzealous "fan." He encourages me when my ego has taken a beating and talks me down when I become too full of myself. While he never fails to praise me when I've delivered a good performance, he also has no problem telling me when I've fallen short of my goals. He really seems to enjoy being a force "behind the scenes" in show business.

*Ringing in Y2K together on New Year's Eve 1999*

A close friend of ours once observed, "You guys are a perfect match! Leon only likes to talk on stage, and Laurence likes to talk everywhere else."

I'm not easy to please, nor easy to understand. Yet Laurence doesn't lose his patience or temper nearly as often as he probably *should*.

This wasn't always the case. Our first few years were filled with some furious fights, as this uptight, withholding WASP learned how to adjust to life with a big, bossy Jew! I would chafe against what I then interpreted as attempts to "control" me. He'd explode when I'd spend too much money. Laurence's brother witnessed some of those battles and joked that our door frames would need constant repainting, given how often and how hard we slammed doors when we fought.

We eventually found a wonderful couples therapist, ironically named "Dr. Ruth," who really helped us learn how to disagree without screaming – too much!

We still sometimes argue with … gusto! So much so, we now have a "safe word" – "jabberwocky" – when things get too heated. Just another part of learning to fight fair. But we must enjoy arguing on some level, because we've never employed that safe word during a fight. Not once, no matter how passionate the disagreement.

We have adjusted to each other's idiosyncrasies. I quickly learned not to be offended when he eats off my plate. When I discover multiple TVs playing in different rooms, I just switch them off without a lecture. He grew accustomed to my clutter and disorganization. He's discovered that my tendency *not* to share feelings isn't about him, but due to my lack of experience at sharing them. And he's learned perhaps the most important fact there is to know about me: Nothing makes me *less* calm than hearing the words "Calm down."

So despite being in a "successful, long-term marriage," I'm always a bit surprised when people ask me for the "secrets" of a successful, long-term marriage! I usually reply, "How the hell would I know? We just figure it out as we go!" Frankly, I'm at a loss as to why we've been successful (particularly during the past three years), while others who seem more inclined to marriage have failed.

So I'm sorry. I have no secrets to share. I don't even know if there *is* a secret.

However, here are a few things that certainly help:

### 1. Luck

Based upon my own experience, I know that "luck" is the biggest "secret" there is. But it's not something you can create or develop. You either have it, or you don't. Thank God, back in 1992, I still had some. I was very lucky to meet Laurence. And I know it, based on all the others I met before him (that I *wasn't* so lucky with)!

### 2. Separate closets

I am pretty meticulous about my clothes and how I arrange them in my closet.[22] Laurence, on the other hand, will allow his dry-cleanables to gather in piles in the corner at the bottom of his closet. Sometimes just looking at the heaps inside his messy closet makes me anxious. So I keep my mouth shut and

---

[22] Not quite *Mommie Dearest*, though, as I use wire hangers.

let him "do him" – at least until I discover something of *mine* I'd thought was long lost buried on his closet floor.

Which brings us to my next tip:

### 3. Pick Your Battles

We often overlook little irritants in friends. That's how we maintain our friendships. So why can't we be that nice to our spouses? Try to overlook the truly menial. If you think about it, aren't *most* of our domestic fights based on menial disagreements or misunderstandings that just build up over time? So let him think he *didn't* forget to run the dishwasher. And maybe he won't remind you that *you* forgot to unload it!

### 4. Fight Constructively

Sometimes, you simply cannot overlook your partner's behavior. As the old saying goes, "You have to break some eggs to make an omelet."

As odd as it seems to see this as a tip to a long-lasting marriage, it's true! The trick is, you *must* learn to fight fair. No name calling. No "punching below the belt." No casual dropping of the word "divorce." Get mad. Get it out. Then get over it.

Laurence can recover from an argument within seconds. It takes me much longer. Conversely, sometimes Laurence can take hours to see his mistakes. Long story short – we've learned *not* to try to patch things up quickly. One must feel what one feels until one feels something else.

And to facilitate that –

## 5. Separate bedrooms

It's easier said than done. But if you can afford it, it is well worth the investment. If not, utilize a guest room. It's always a good idea to have a "room of one's own." (Just ask Virginia Woolf.) You don't have to sleep separately. Just have "separate corners" to which to retreat.

And if you're lucky enough to stay together a *really* long time, you might actually graduate to sleeping separately.

About 10 years ago, due to mutual sleep issues, Laurence and I were driving each other crazy in the bedroom, and *not* in a good way! He prefers to fall asleep with the TV on, while I require silence and complete darkness. I tossed and turned and spread out like a swastika.[23] I would snap awake at the slightest sound or movement. Meanwhile, Laurence used to snore like a buzz saw, and occasionally suffered from acid reflux. We eventually realized that if we were to ever get recuperative sleep, we'd *have* to sleep separately.

Since then, my issues have settled. Thanks to (safe) medication, I now sleep much more soundly. Laurence has learned techniques that have almost eliminated his snoring completely. At this point, though, we're so set in our ways that we *almost* always sleep in our separate beds – but only after tucking each other in each night.

Yes, it used to bug me a little. Then I remembered my grandparents, married over 75 years, had separate bedrooms since I was a kid, too. Don't knock it until you try it!

---

[23] I wish I could take credit for that line, but I stole it from Clare Booth Luce's play *The Women*.

### 6. Separate bathrooms

Naturally, not every couple can afford two bathrooms. In fact, we've only pulled it off twice, during particularly flush periods of our lives. But man, what a joy mornings were back in those days! No jockeying for the shower, or toilet, or sink, when both of us were trying to get ready for work at the same time.

If battling for bathroom time is a cause of conflict in your home, you should seriously look at your budget and figure out how to upsize a little. And then, use the time you save to share a cup of coffee together before starting your day.

### 7. Selective, Short-Term Memory Loss

Who doesn't like to be a "know it all"? I do! God knows, at times, I've practically made a career of it!

But when it comes to a long-term relationship, you need to know when to "get stupid." When to keep your big mouth shut. It just doesn't pay to always be all-wise and all-knowing. Stop saying "You always…" and "You never…". Avoid all sentences that begin with "Didn't I tell you that …" or "If you'd listened to me to begin with …" or especially "I knew that you would…" and "I told you so!"

You know you both mean well, right? You truly don't have to remind each other of just how many times you've disappointed each other.

Do you?

# Why Do We Love Divas? Let Us Count the Ways

"My son isn't gay! He loves women!"
The women:

Maybe it started with Greta Garbo. Quentin Crisp was a huge fan.

If you're older than I am – admit it or not, some of you are – perhaps Judy Garland is your goddess. Guys around my age love Streisand, Midler, Joan Collins, Madonna. And if you're younger than I am, maybe its Beyoncé or Lady Gaga or Britney Spears or (God forbid) Taylor Swift.

The list of divas who have won the love, respect, and support of gay men grows longer all the time. Even the butchest gay man can turn nelly over Liza Minnelli. So if it's not a generational thing, what is it about strong female entertainers that speaks to most gay men?

Writer David-Elijah Nahmod claims that Cher "tells me that it's OK to be who I am."

Mitchell Troy loves Bette Davis because "she did things her way. She never minced words. If she liked you, she liked you. If she didn't, you knew it! She had a huge career and an interesting life."

Many of our divas stand the test of time. For example, Garland is still #1 diva for many, including twenty-something actor Charles William Romaine. "She basically invented the multi-hyphenate career and set the standard for other performers. Her music and movies continue to attract new audiences. As Frank Sinatra famously said, 'The rest of us will be forgotten. Never Judy.'"

Tallulah Bankhead is Jerry Linkhart's diva-of-choice. Why? "While President Truman was visiting her suite, she had a call to nature. She insisted on leaving the door open while peeing so she wouldn't miss anything! Plus, she slept with both Hattie McDaniel and Billie Holiday!"

Some of our divas are less obvious. Johnny Kat of San Francisco cites Cass Elliot as his favorite. "When she sang 'Different is hard, different is lonely, different is trouble for you only. Different is heartache, different is pain. But I'd rather be different than be the same,' she was speaking directly to me," says Kat.

Television supplied many women for young gay boys to worship. Some grew up idolizing fictional television divas Lucy Ricardo, Samantha and Endora of *Bewitched*; or Jeannie of *I Dream of Jeannie*. For me, it was watching *The Bionic Woman* played by Lindsay Wagner and Lynda Carter's *Wonder Woman*. Younger generations have embraced Alexis

Carrington, *Zena the Warrior Princess*, *Buffy the Vampire Slayer*, and Valerie Cherish of *The Comeback*.

It's often been speculated that *Golden Girls* is really about gay men, played by women. The same has been said for *Absolutely Fabulous* and *Sex and the City*. Maybe, as some believe, older gay men prefer their stories be told with women in our roles; perhaps it's easier to digest than a "mirror image" of ourselves?

Then again, perhaps it's the "survivor" we recognize and identify with. Many of our favorite divas have taken hit after hit, only to bounce back, bigger and better than ever. Gay men certainly take their share of hard knocks in life – maybe we identify with their resilience?

Or perhaps it's because our divas have supported us, even before it was acceptable to do so publicly. Joan Crawford had a long friendship with gay actor-turned-designer William Hayes. Tallulah is quoted as saying "There's a bit of the homosexual in all of us, don't you know."

Recently, Dolly Parton took her country-western fans to task for judging gays. Lisa Kudrow stated in a recent interview that she felt gay men were "superior" beings.

And of course, Elizabeth Taylor out-diva'd them all. Always an advocate of the gay community ("there would be no Hollywood without gays"), she came out swinging against AIDS before any of her contemporaries – becoming as famous for her support of LGBTQ as she was for her glittering film career, breathtaking jewels, many marriages, and battles against substance abuse.

I think the answer goes even deeper.

Whether fictional or real life, there are two things all these women had or have in common: extraordinary talent and incredible strength.

Back in my 20s, I asked my then-shrink: Why would I, a gay man and non-violent pacifist, grow up worshiping ass-kickers like Bionic Woman and Wonder Woman? Why did these two role models strike such a chord with me when I was a kid?

His reply was so quick and simple, I'm embarrassed I'd never thought of it before.

He explained, "As a kid, you sought strong role models who were still capable of compassion and fear. So you identified with Jamie Sommers, who felt fear but did the job anyway, and Diana Prince, who could kick ass but fought to establish peace. Male heroes are macho. Machoism goes hand in hand with homophobia. Being gay, you wanted heroes without all that macho bullshit attached."

It made sense to me, and still does. Whether their gifts are witchcraft, super-human strength, a great singing voice, stinging wit, or a constitution strong enough to endure multiple divorces and/or numerous overdoses, our heroines are capable and strong. And none of them – from Bette and Tallulah to Cher and Buffy – come with any "homophobic machismo bullshit" attached.

Speaking of favorite divas…

# Why Wonder Woman?

*Obsession + Hot-Glue Gun = Favorite Halloween Costume Ever*

Since childhood, this gay man's diva of choice has been DC Comics' Wonder Woman, created by Dr. William Moulton Marston over 80 years ago.

Famed comic-book writer/artist George Perez, who chronicled Wonder Woman in the 1980s, describes her thusly: "...a star-spangled amalgam of fantasy, American patriotism, ancient myth, science fiction, and even a not-so-subtle hint of kinkiness."

I'm frequently asked, *Why Wonder Woman?*

It's a question I've pondered a lot over the decades. Alas, there isn't one simple answer.

As a gay kid, I wanted a role model who exhibited strength without asshole-ism. That's certainly one reason. I could write an entire book just unpacking *that* theory. But this is about her, not me!

Another reason I identified with Diana was her backstory.

Here's someone with a charmed life – a princess, no less – living in such a utopia that it was literally named "Paradise Island." (The name "Themyscira" came later.)

Yet despite this blessed existence, Diana felt restless and longed for more – to experience life in "Man's World," to use her talents and skills for a greater good. So she left paradise behind and journeyed to a brand-new world. (Unlike Superman and Batman, she could still return home to family when she wanted or needed to.)

I grew up in rural Indiana, which is downright bucolic. Yet for as long as I can remember, I longed to leave it behind, to move to the "big city," to experience different lifestyles and cultures – so long as I could come back home to visit!

As soon as I read my very first *Wonder Woman* comic book, how I wished for an invisible jet of my own, that would allow me to live in both worlds.

And then there's her status as an LGBTQ icon. Long before I ever heard the term "gender roles," I relished how Diana Prince turned sexual stereotypes and conventions on their heads.[24]

Diana came from a land of only women. She advocated equality. She loved Steve Trevor but refused to "settle down"

---

[24] Her creator Marston certainly defied convention with his polyamorous home life – but that's yet another book.

and get married because doing so would only distract her from her life's work.

Most importantly, she was never the "damsel in distress," waiting to be rescued by a man. *She* was the cavalry, constantly saving Trevor's ass.[25]

I enjoyed the *SuperFriends* cartoon. But once the TV show starring Lynda Carter debuted in 1975, this 12-year-old was a deeply committed fanatic. The series fell apart a bit after it moved to CBS and was updated to the 1970s, but its first season on ABC – set during World War II in the 1940s – remained perhaps the most faithful adaptation of an original comic-book property to TV or film until *Watchmen*. And Lynda Carter-as-Wonder Woman may be the most ideal Hollywood casting since Vivien Leigh won the role of Scarlett O'Hara in *Gone with the Wind*.

I'm sure I'm not the only gay boy who spun himself dizzy back then, emulating her explosive costume change.

From my earliest exposure to the comic books, I also appreciated that Wonder Woman's mission set her apart from all the other spandexed superheroes and made her truly unique.

She wasn't the world's greatest detective, out to strike terror in the hearts of criminals, like Bats.

She wasn't the guardian of the universe and enforcer of truth and justice, like Superman.

She wasn't thrust into her role by events outside her control – like the demise of her planet, or murder of her parents, or a bite from a radioactive spider. She *chose* to be the hero.

---

[25] Her earliest stories also contained a good deal of "bondage and discipline" – something I never picked up on until I was an adult!

And unlike her "Bam! Pow!" colleagues, Wonder Woman used force and might as a last resort. She almost always saw the potential for good in even the worst villains and preferred to resolve conflicts with truth and reason instead of fisticuffs.

Many early Wonder Woman tales didn't end with the criminal going to jail because Diana was just as interested in forgiveness, redemption, and transformation. She felt anyone could change for the better and even convinced vile Nazi Baroness Paula von Gunther to change her evil ways and use her genius for the good of humanity. (After a stint at the Amazons' "Transformation Island," Gunther became Paradise Island's leading scientist.)

And that really appealed to this young pacifist!

Unfortunately, the "pacifist warrior" aspect of her character can be particularly vexing for some of her writers and can make creating an exciting conclusion to a Wonder Woman tale especially challenging. (Don't believe me? Just watch the frustrating *Wonder Woman 1984*.) Perhaps this is why the character was revamped by DC Comics in the mid-1980s.

After a wonderful start with the aforementioned writer/artist Perez, this new Wonder Woman began to embrace her warrior heritage. She often carried a sword and a shield. Her desire to reform criminals was toned down in favor of a more brutal Amazon. Idyllic Paradise Island became strive-filled Themyscira.

As comics in general became darker, she seemed to stray further from her pacifist roots. The "point of no return" came in 2005, when Wonder Woman snapped the neck of villain Maxwell Lord. (Granted, I found myself wishing she'd do just that by the end of *Wonder Woman 1984*!)

Around this time, I stopped reading her monthly adventures. The "New 52" interpretation of the character was just too violent to take, and too much of a departure from the character I grew up loving. Over the years, I sold off my massive collection of comic books and most of my action figures and statues.

*Just part of my collection, circa 2005, when it filled a small room*

But I never gave up on Marston's original heroine, the peace-loving character I grew up with. So I was thrilled in 2017 when the long-awaited, well-received feature film *Wonder Woman* restored a bit of that original sense of the character. I was even more thrilled that Patty Jenkins and Gal Gadot brought her a new level of respect and appreciation, especially since she spent many of her decades languishing – suffering from creative teams that didn't "get" her, constant revamps of origin and character, and a publishing company that often treated her as an afterthought.

DC isn't making that mistake these days. They've since jettisoned most of the "New 52" and have brought the character a bit closer to her original incarnation. DC finally reveres her as much as Superman and Batman since her big box-office debut.

Now if only they'd get rid of that damned sword and shield!

# Blond on *Blonde*

One judges "entertainment" by standards like "Did you laugh? Did you cry? Did you forget about life while watching?"

"Art," however, is held to stricter standards. Does it stick with you? Does it haunt you afterwards? Did it disturb you? Does it go someplace new and daring? Can two people look at it but see two different things?

*Blonde*, Netflix's recent contribution to the ever-growing collection of films about Marilyn Monroe, is a gigantic flop when judged as an "entertainment." There are just too many things to hate about it.

But – God help me – even with all its warts, indulgences, and over-the-top ugliness, the film *does* qualify as art.

If you're one of the thousands who reportedly turned it off at the 20-minute mark, you must admit that you didn't quickly forget your experience. *Did you?*

I fully expected to be one of those viewers who switched it off in disgust. After all, I only tuned in to see what the fuss was all about. And while I did take a break (to catch my breath and take an Ativan), I did turn it back on. Because visually, it is the most remarkable, breathtaking, and audacious film I have seen in a long, long time.

The massive negative reaction is partially Netflix's own fault. They were wrong to promote this picture as a biopic.

Because, even with her childhood, marriages, and many film roles depicted, this is *not* Marilyn Monroe's life story. It is based on a *novel* by Joyce Carol Oates – a work of fiction – and not on any Monroe biography.

This is not the Marilyn we know – certainly not the Marilyn we *think* we know. Director Andrew Dominik wants us to feel how Marilyn saw and felt about herself. This is Marilyn from the inside looking out, not Marilyn from the outside looking in.

This is the fever dream of a mentally ill, increasingly drug-addled woman who felt exploited and betrayed at every turn. On that level, it succeeds marvelously – maybe too well.

Ultimately, *Blonde* is an unrelenting horror film. A monster movie. And the monster is the multi-headed hydra of Hollywood. The "haunted house" is sexist 1950s America. "Toxic masculinity" is the character you hope will save the heroine but who ultimately betrays her. And Marilyn is the horror film's "Final Girl," who survives all the attacks and horrors and indignities. Well, except that [spoiler alert!] she dies at the end.

Ana de Armas' performance is amazing and truly deserves to be seen – *if* you're up to the challenge. The production itself is absolutely breathtaking to look at. The combination of different film stocks & ratios, the mixing of color with black & white, the occasional distortion of the images, and moments of reality twisting with dreams and hallucinations – it's as if the film *Frances* had been written by David Lynch, directed by Baz Luhrmann, and produced by Russ Meyer.

All that said, there *is* a lot in this movie that turns the stomach.

A talking fetus shames Marilyn for having an abortion? I get that it's just happening in her head. But given today's heated culture, it's easily misinterpreted as an anti-abortion message, instead of just Monroe's damaged "inner monologue." I found the sequence wildly irresponsible and designed merely to provoke – especially by using images of a fetus to do so.

Audiences particularly hate a scene late in the third act, wherein President Kennedy forces Marilyn to perform oral sex. It *is* extremely graphic, outside the bounds of good taste, and perhaps the hardest scene of all to watch. But I have no trouble imagining their relationship playing out in that fashion, with Secret Service men sitting just outside the open bedroom door.

What about the "Big Question"? Did Kennedy have her killed? Dominik tries to have it both ways. There's a nightmare-ish moment, shortly after her presidential rape, where she awakens in the middle of the night to find trench-coated G-men tearing her place apart. She hides under the sheets. They come for her. And as this scene plays out, you assume "Oh, here we are, this is 'The End.'"

But that turns out to be a nightmare – *or was it?* Soon enough, we then watch her washing down too many pills with straight booze, and taking to her bed, after receiving (completely made up) bad news. Given how fucking ballsy the film is up until then, and all the legitimate real-life questions surrounding her death, this dénouement feels more than a bit cowardly.

There's good reason why some critics are calling it "torture porn." Jesus Christ, are we to believe there wasn't a single moment of joy in the poor woman's life? Never a moment of clarity? Not a second of self-realization?

The film is also loaded with falsehoods which will enrage fans familiar with her true story, but again, it was based on a novel, *not* her actual life.

I certainly recommend this film to hard-core film buffs without hesitation because it's an amazing visual spectacle and is incredibly edited and mixed. But hard-core Monroe fans? Think long and hard before strapping in for this trip.

Does the film deserve the backlash? Frankly, I've seen much worse. Darren Aronofsky's 2017 shit show *Mother!* is far more offensive, and not at all successful artistically. *In the Realm of the Senses* or, hell, even *Showgirls* were much more painful for me to watch.

Sadly, it didn't have to be this way. The film could have, and *should* have, opened with a disclaimer that it was based on a work of *fiction* that was merely *inspired* by Monroe's life. But no.

In the credits, DiMaggio is called "The Former Athlete." Arthur Miller is called "The Playwright" and Kennedy is "The President." Perhaps Dominik should've used that approach with Marilyn herself, and just called her "The Blonde." If he'd made the movie more of a *roman à clef* or given it the *Citizen Kane* treatment (which was *still* about William Randolph Hearst even though the character was named Charles Foster Kane), perhaps her legion of fans could better tolerate the wild liberties and outrageous exaggerations.

Just another way Netflix *could've* made it less offensive to Marilyn's fans.

It's a shame. Because there is a lot of gold in this gutter.

But I write this not to change minds. You'll either love it or hate it (or, like me, you'll love *and* hate it). And whatever your reaction, you are 100% correct.

And isn't that what "art" is all about?

# Tech Kills: A Partial Casualty List

"New York City is no longer the Island of Misfit Toys," my friend Erik complained recently. "It doesn't have to be. Not anymore. Not since we all have one of *these*."

He lifted his phone from the table and held it as if it were radioactive.

No, he wasn't extolling the benefits and virtues of technology. Rather, he was complaining about how it had changed the LGBTQ community in Manhattan.

If you're our age or older (and still breathing), you probably remember how teachers told us that one day, within our lifetimes, home computers – *home computers!* – would eliminate most chores. As a result, they promised, daily life would become a breeze!

Those teachers also told us America was about to adopt the metric system, so we'd better learn it quick!

Okay, I'll just say it. Our teachers lied. On both accounts.

They did get *one* thing right: Computers are now omnipresent. No longer content with computers just in our homes and businesses, we now carry them in our pockets or wrapped around our wrists.

But has life truly become easier as a result?

That prediction, it turns out, was as bogus as the threat of milligrams and kilometers.

Yes, we can buy groceries – or anything else for that matter – without leaving our homes. We download music, watch movies, read news, play games, text each other instantly, share our innermost thoughts with the entire world via social media, all without ever lifting our asses up off the couch.

But is it really worth it? Is it worth the intrusion, the loss of privacy, the loss of so much human interaction, just for the immediacy of – well, *everything*?

Younger generations may sadly never know that delicious agony of waiting weeks for something they really want, or that sweet release when it finally arrived. Not in the era of instant gratification and "same-day delivery."

Young lovers will never experience the exquisite heartache of waiting by the mailbox for a highly anticipated love letter to arrive. Not when they can email and text (and sext) instantly.

I feel sad for anyone who's never experienced a lazy Sunday afternoon curled up with a book or listening to an album on vinyl from start to finish, without looking at a phone or a screen.

Or anyone who hasn't had to wait three whole days to see the photos they just took.

"Wait a minute," you may say. "Aren't you biting the hand that fed you? After all, *you* owe your biggest success as an actor to the internet and technology!"

Yes. The internet *has* made it easier for artists to get their work made and seen. I left Indiana in the mid-1980s to pursue a life in show business. Nowadays, the series *Canary Currency* is shot in my hometown of Kokomo. So yes, creating art does feel a bit more "democratic" now that anyone can make it and share it.

But there *is* a downside. Making a traditional living as an entertainment professional has never been more challenging – unless you have a million followers on social media or are willing to go the OnlyFans route.

I sound like a grumpy old queen again, don't I?

So instead of just generally wailing about the futuristic shape of things, here's a list of ten victims of technology that I mourn the most.

### 1.  Print Media (Newspapers, magazines, etc.)

Since I'm a news junkie, you'd think I'd enjoy accessing news 24/7. I *used* to. But since 2020, I've been asking myself: Do we *really* need to know everything that happens the instant it occurs? Are our brains wired to handle so much information? So much stress? Is it healthy to know about horrors half-a-world away when we can do nothing but watch?

I still get the *Los Angeles Times* and read it daily. I like the feel of the paper in my hands, turning the pages. But I'm in a rapidly shrinking minority. As a result of cable and internet news, local newspapers are dead and dying. The larger "big city" papers are getting thinner and thinner by the year. No matter how popular MSNBC and CNN may be, you'll never get the same in-depth news coverage from talking heads that print media offers.

Frankly, I'd love far less opinion and much more actual coverage. I think our country might grow a bit less divided as a result. But those news channels make money from high ratings, and nothing promotes viewership as successfully as anger and outrage.

And don't get me started on how much I miss "movie magazines" like *Premiere*, *Film Threat*, and *Movieline*.

Speaking of print…

## 2. Bookstores

Yes, e-books are great for the environment. Yes, it's pretty cool to order a book and get it the very next day (*if* you don't feel bad for that delivery person who is breaking her back to get it to you).

But good God, how I miss spending long afternoons leisurely browsing stacks at bookstores. If nothing else, they offered hours of free entertainment, so long as you didn't buy anything (something I could never *not* do!). It was a great way to discover new authors, find new hobbies, and even meet new friends.

Yes, Amazon lets you see the back cover, and peek inside at the first few pages. But it's just not the same sensory experience. I want to smell the pages. I want to feel the covers (high gloss? matte?) in my hands. I want to be lured to check out that book just because of the color on the spine, or the font of the title.

If you're lucky enough to *still* have a bookstore in your neighborhood or town, I beg you to go there *now* and buy something!

## 3. Video Stores

I understand younger generations are more interested in "experiences" than "possessions." And why take up space storing blu-rays or DVDs when streaming is so popular and convenient and doesn't require storage?

But there *is* a cost.

Gone are the days when you could discover an obscure title you'd never heard of at the video store. Similarly, also gone are the days when you could stumble upon a late-night movie on TV. Looking for your favorite cult film? Good luck finding *Liquid Sky* or *Puzzle of a Downfall Child* or *Echo Park* on any of the major streaming platforms!

Home video was also a good source of back-end financing for independent filmmakers back in the day. Then *poof!* Streamers do pay, but not as much as old-fashioned video did.

A desperate few stores are still hanging on by a thread, like "Vidiots" in Santa Monica. But John Waters summarized it best when he said that video stores destroyed midnight movies, and now streaming has all but destroyed video stores.

### 4. Record Stores

Much like book and video stores, I miss discovering new artists, or rediscovering old favorites, at record stores – particularly at *used* record stores (which were very popular in San Francisco back in the day). Like book stores, you could spend entire afternoons reading liner notes and never spend a dime. Or, you could walk out with a stack of vinyl for only a few dollars. I fear the few that still exist, like Amoeba Music in Hollywood, are not long for this world.

### 5. Taxis

I guess Uber and Lyft are cool, if for no other reason than it allows folks to earn quick money. But I miss the spontaneity of spotting a cab, deciding in a split-second whether it's worth the expense, and hailing it down. It was the closest I've ever come to playing a sport.

Taxi drivers were also much more fearless in traffic than that college student who just picked you up. Ever tell an Uber driver, "There's an extra $20 in it for you if you can get me to the airport in 15 minutes"? No, I didn't think so.

The only benefit of Uber is that the back seats smell a lot nicer. Or at least they're supposed to.

### 6. Gay Bars

Believe it or not, gay bars were about much more than cruising (and that's pretty much gone, too). Bars were about community building, about finding our tribe. A place to be yourself without fear. A place to celebrate with friends without worry or judgment. And yes, cruising that cute guy at the pool table, too!

I suppose Grindr is cool if you're looking for a quick hook-up with a minimum of fuss. But I wouldn't use it even if I were single. I'd find it kind of odd to enter a restaurant and have everyone know my business before I even sit down.

I prefer the old-fashioned way of eyes meeting across a crowded room, and then...

### 7. Mom and Pop Stores

Alas, "big box" stores were killing these well before Amazon put the final nails in the coffins, so I can't blame only Jeff Bezos here.

I also can't point fingers. I shop on Amazon, too. And chances are good, you bought this very book there, too.

But I draw the line at self-checkout at the grocery store or Target. Self-checkout is the devil. Do you use them? Shame on you.

## 8. Water-Cooler Moments

Back when "legacy networks" were the only game in town, Americans bonded over our shared viewing experiences and talked about them the next day at school or work "around the water cooler" (thus the expression).

I remember the shared excitement, back when I was a kid, as we discovered the *entire country* tuned in to the miniseries *Roots*, or how we *all* attended "Rhoda's wedding." I still remember squealing with delight with my fellow comic-book-loving sixth graders the morning after the *Wonder Woman* TV pilot debuted.

With streaming platforms and hundreds of cable channels, those days died a long time ago. We've been splintered into hundreds of channels and a dozen (and counting) streamers.

Would "Who Shot J.R.?" have been a phenomenon in today's TV landscape? No way!

Water coolers are still a thing, aren't they?

## 9. Human Courtesy

How can we make eye contact when everyone is looking down at their phones? How do spontaneous conversations happen if we all have buds stuck in our ears? Can we ever find middle ground when it's so easy to attack one another on social media without consequence? How often have I thought "What a rude bitch!" when I haven't received a reply or acknowledgment after saying "hello" to someone. Then I look at their ears. Yep. Another zombie lost to technology.

**10. Privacy**

The highest cost of all. Oddly, many give it away without even realizing it. I'm always amazed when folks who should know better take those "What Kind of Flower Am I?" and "What Color Am I?" quizzes on Facebook.

Have you ever had a conversation about buying an item, then ads for that very item start popping up on your social-media feeds? I have, more than once. And it gives me the willies.

I know Alexa says she doesn't eavesdrop. I don't believe the lying bitch. She knows too much.

That's my top ten, but there's so much more I miss from the "good old days."

Do you recall the deep satisfaction of ending an angry phone call by slamming the heavy receiver down onto its plastic cradle? Gone.

I miss calling a travel agent and having them deal with the tedious details. Gone.

I never thought I'd miss trying to read a map or looking something up in the World Book Encyclopedia. But I do.

How I long for the days of Top 40 Radio.

So many things have been discarded in the name of modernity.

I only hope democracy doesn't become one of them…

# Closets Are for Costumes

Anytime an established actor comes out of the closet, he or she (or they) should be applauded. It's a brave thing to do in Hollywood. Not only are they confronting the prejudices of Middle America, but chances are they're also disappointing resistant agents, facing the prejudices of homophobic producers and casting directors, and maybe even risking financial ruin. It takes a lot of guts.

That said, I reserve my biggest admiration for actors who were never in the closet to begin with. To me, those are the true heroes. The trailblazers. As difficult as the acting profession is, starting out with no secrets is truly an act of courage.

Alas, most gay actors still remain closeted. And it's not always the result of self-loathing or external homophobia. When young actors start out, most are determined – *nay*, desperate – to be what the "powers that be" want, not who they really are. They want to fit in. They train away their accents, transform themselves at the gym, get their ears nipped or their noses done.

They're too inexperienced to realize it's not what makes you blend in that counts, but what makes you stand out.

I'm not advocating showing up at auditions in a T-shirt that reads, "Why, yes, I am!" There's no need to attend that film premiere carrying a picket sign. But you must be brave enough, when asked, to answer the question honestly. Because if you refuse to answer the question, you've *answered* the question. After all, do you know any straight men who hesitate to declare their love for women? I don't.

Remember Ricky Martin's awkward interview with Barbara Walters? His refusal to answer her question was confirmation to most, and many mocked him for his timidity. It took years for his career to recover, but it did – after he came out.

I've worked with closeted actors playing gay roles, and the experience is exasperating, to say the least. It's not like they fool anyone with all the genderless pronouns. Their endless declarations that they are "nothing at all like the character" get on my last gay nerve.

They'll tell you they don't want to be "labeled." That's an admirable goal. The world would be a lovely place if people didn't label each other. I hope to live long enough to see that world. But we aren't there yet.

In my opinion, the only way we'll do away with labels, ironically, is to first label everything. Only when the easily titillated see that LGBTQ are everywhere, that we come in all sizes, colors, and variations, and that most of us are just as boring as they are, will they tire of playing "Who's gay?"

That's one reason why coming out is so important.

"I never said I was a role model" is another retort I've heard from defensive closeted actors. Another gutless cop-out, if you ask me. Like it or not, actors have a responsibility beyond themselves. Most of us become actors because we want to represent the underrepresented. I've always felt being an actor is similar to being an elected official. (For example, I am representing all the middle-aged, pencil-necked gay geeks.)

Actors act to promote understanding, to improve the human condition – at least that's why *good* ones do it! If you're only in it for fame, fortune, and ego gratification, get out.

There *are* some jobs where it makes good sense to keep your sexuality secret – a small-town school teacher, for example, or a soldier in the military. But show business, despite some of its old-school tendencies, is one of the most liberal industries on the planet. And it's getting better for out actors. Jim Parsons was the star of TV's top sitcom, for which he's won four Emmys. Zachary Quinto had a lead role in a huge film franchise, where he not only got big fight scenes but also won "the girl." Neil Patrick Harris, Alan Cumming, Billy Porter, Matt Bomer, Cheyenne Jackson. The list gets longer all the time.

Alas, despite the progress we have made in the battle for equal rights, we are far from finished. There are still too many young gay people growing up surrounded by hatred, and they need to see well-adjusted, successful queer folk who thrive without fear. There are too many ignorant bigots who also need to see us in all our glorious diversity. Once they do, then maybe we really will do away with those labels.

I will stop preaching and allow Mr. Webster to have the final word:

> "**Courage** (noun): the ability to do something that you know is difficult or dangerous; mental or moral strength to venture, persevere, and withstand danger, fear, or difficulty"

# Critical, Darling

Ah, critics. Many in show business hate them, some claim to ignore them, but there's no denying that critics are a necessary evil in this industry – just imagine trying to sell a play or film without reviews!

Granted, many critics and their write-ups aren't very useful beyond promoting (or killing) a production. You'll often learn more about the reviewers – their likes and dislikes – than about the quality of the shows they critique.

And critics aren't invulnerable. Despite all evidence to the contrary, they *are* human. Bad weather, a lousy dinner, crappy seats, an argument with the spouse, constipation – all can be the true reasons behind a negative review.

As for those artists who say they never read their reviews? I'm not so sure I believe them. Surely some of them *must* be telling the truth. And those actors/writers/producers/directors who truly don't read their notices, in my humble opinion, are missing out.

Because there really are some very good, astute critics. And while I would never alter a performance based upon any review, the more intelligent write-ups are a great way for an actor (or director or playwright) to learn how their work is being perceived and if the show is hitting its intended mark.

The best critics, like Roger Ebert or Pauline Kael, elevated critique into an art form. Their opinions were so revered, they've been compiled and published in book form.

And then there are critics like *San Francisco Chronicle*'s Mick LaSalle. He finds himself so fascinating he once took up half a page of valuable newspaper space to talk about what makes *him* tick.

These days, the internet is stuffed with self-proclaimed culture "experts." It seems *everyone* is a critic. A few are very good. But all the mediocre ones have diminished both the value of reviews and the role of legitimate critics.

If all your reviews are raves, you can assume you're delivering the goods. If all the notices are pans, you must assume the opposite.

If you believe the good ones, you are obligated to believe the bad ones, too.

And if you're a "sub-lebrity" like me, and an unproven commodity in terms of "box office," getting consistently good reviews allows you to claim that you're at least a *critical* success!

Back in 2010, I was twiddling my thumbs at home instead of strutting my stuff on stage. So I was intrigued when Ryan Gierach, then editor-in-chief of West Hollywood's online newspaper *WeHo News*, asked me to join his staff as his theatre critic.

"You love writing, and you love theatre. What better use of my talents could there be?" argued the practical half of my Gemini brain.

*"But you're an actor!"* screamed the other, more melodramatic half in reply. *"What if you pan a show then find yourself auditioning for that show's director or playwright down the road? Or end up sharing a dressing room with an actor you've previously trashed? You love to burn bridges, Leon, but is it smart to torch them* before *you cross them?"*

"Well, your stage career isn't exactly in the stratosphere, is it? You don't even have a day job right now. At least this will keep you in touch with what's going on in Los Angeles theatre!" I told myself.

*"But those who can, do. Those who can't, teach. And those who can't teach, write reviews!"*

Not completely convinced, I finally told Ryan I'd give it a shot.

At first it was pretty uneventful. I averaged a show a week, and most of the plays I saw were neither brilliant nor horrible, and I forgot about them as soon as I emailed Ryan my copy.

It began to dawn on me: There may be a lot of theatre in Los Angeles, but very little of it was truly outstanding or memorable. Quantity doesn't equal quality. I was now beginning to understand why *Back Stage* editor Dany Margoles had once thanked me for "creating high-quality theatre" after *Carved in Stone* had closed.

I also began to realize that *not* working constantly on Hollywood's stages wasn't necessary a bad thing, after all. At least I was avoiding appearing in a lot of clunkers. I realized how damned lucky I was that the shows in which I *had* been cast were all, more or less, critically successful.

Every so often, a gem would present itself for review.

*Mystery of Irma Vep*, masterfully directed by Michael Lorre and (coincidentally) starring my brilliant *Carved in Stone* co-star, the late, great Kevin Remington, still has me marveling at their break-neck pacing.

*How Katrina Plays* by the late Judi Ann Mason, directed by Tchia Casselle at the Write Act Rep, had its audience feeling as though they, too, were stranded in a New Orleans nightclub as the hurricane bore down upon them.

*Scarcity* by Lucy Thurber, directed by Kappy Kilburn at the Imagined Life Theatre, told the story of a teacher's attempts to "rescue" her brilliant student from his troubled, blue-collar home-life. It featured "should-be-star turns" by Jarrett Sleeper and Kim Swennen.

But those were the exceptions.

One night found me in a small, gloomy "black box" in the worst part of Hollywood, watching – well, it's over a decade later and I *still* don't know what the fuck *that* show was about.

It seemed to have been made up as it went along. First, it's a family drama. Then it's a coming-out story. Then it's a tale about the challenge of American immigrants. Then the mom is suddenly dead, and now it's a father-son buddy comedy. Wait! Did the son just confess he feels he's a woman trapped in a man's body?

What it continued to morph into during the second act I cannot tell you, as I walked out at intermission – and declined to write about it.

To paraphrase the advice my mom often offered, if you can't say anything nice, say nothing at all.

Alas, I didn't follow her advice for long.

I eventually reviewed a show called *Hellz Kitchen Ablaze*. I was already suspicious going in, as the show's promotional material declared the show's director, David Fofi (whom I'd never heard of), was "the hot director of the moment."

*Yeah, sure, okay.*

Clearly inspired by *The Sopranos* (then at its peak), playwright Tommy Carter's drama featured eight hardened Manhattan narcotics officers gathering to mourn the accidental shooting death of one of their own after a drug bust gone awry.

Oh, to hell with it. I'll let this paragraph from my review explain the rest:

> The result feels like one of those overly long yet painfully unentertaining *Saturday Night Live* sketches, one spoofing all the clichés of David Mamet, cops on the take, and New York Italians ... 'Sounds like Ellis Island on a good day,' one of the badge-wearing Guidos astutely declares.

Did I go too far?

Apparently one of the actors thought so. Because he immediately emailed my *WeHo Times* editor:

"Hi, my [last] name is 'Parolisi' ... When did it become acceptable to use racial slurs when reviewing an artistic endeavor? 'Guidos' ... Disgraceful. I'm considering legal action."

I explained to Ryan that my use of the slur was intentional and purposeful because all of the characters in the play *were* Italian stereotypes! Ryan then referred Mr. Parolisi to the "letters to the editor" section, saying, "We look forward to you making your case publicly, after all, Leon did."

Alas, Ryan's support would be short-lived, and my days as West Hollywood's Addison DeWitt were about to come crashing to an end.

I invited my friend, actress Amanda Gari, to be my "plus one" for *Broads!*, a musical by Jennie Fahn with music and lyrics by Joe Symon, about four seniors performing one last talent show at their Palm Beach retirement home. Amanda was anxious to see the show, because she had auditioned for it, but was told she was "far too young."

The cast was headlined by noted character actresses June Gable, Leslie Easterbrook, Ivonne Coll, and Barbara Niles. The venue was the venerable El Portal Theatre in North Hollywood. Amanda and I had just enjoyed a wonderful meal, and we had high hopes for a fun, entertaining evening of theatre as we took our seats.

Our hopes were dashed immediately. The show was a flat-out bomb, a turkey, a stinker. Some "highlights" of my review:

> Few things are sadder, theatrically speaking, than watching a talented, likeable cast trying to breathe life into a script that simply does not and will not work ... Symon has squeezed 18 original songs into this 90-minute show. One would think there'd be at least one or two that would stick with you. There isn't ... There's not a single, genuine laugh-out-loud moment.

I know. It sounds very harsh. The show truly was *that* painful.

Songwriter Symon was understandably enraged by my review, and he let Ryan know it repeatedly, via a barrage of phone calls, emails, and Facebook posts. He claimed I trashed the show because Amanda hadn't been cast. He said I was "cruel," "non-objective," "offensive," "venomous and resentful," "unacceptable and appalling." He accused me of conducting a "smear campaign." He claimed my review ignored a "major gay subplot." He told Ryan I was guilty of "abuse of the power by a critic." He suggested I be fired.

Hmmm. Okay, maybe I *did* go too far, I thought. Let's Google reviews of *Broads!* and see what others had written. So I did.

I could not find a single good review. Not one. So I decided to ignore Symon.

That is, until he sent an unbelievably hostile email to me directly, in which he claimed I was so "unhappy about themselves [sic] to the point of lashing out on someone else's project," and that producing *Carved in Stone* had left me bitter and jealous, among other accusations.

*Who the hell does this asshole think he is?*

Ordinarily, I don't believe performers should write to their critics and vice versa. But I had had enough!

Instead of angrily pounding out a bitchy reply, as is my wont, I sat down and composed a professional, three-page "cease-and-desist" letter, in which I destroyed his arguments, one by one.

Regarding the prospect that sour grapes on Amanda's part had colored my review: "If you recall, Ms. Gari was told she was 'far too young for the part.' These are not words that drive an actress to seek 'revenge.'"

Regarding my "ignoring" that "major gay subplot," I pointed out that it is, "in truth, less than five minutes of conversational dialogue sprinkled throughout the play, about a gay son we never see, which leads to no real drama, confrontation, nor resolution ... Your mentioning of this 'glaring oversight' is blatantly an attempt to get attention in a publication with a large gay readership."

Regarding my "lashing out" due to unhappiness with myself and my acting career: "This is absolutely without merit. *Carved in Stone* enjoyed unanimous rave reviews, extended for three months, enjoyed incredible word of mouth, and was embraced by gays and straights alike. ... In fact, it was the highlight of my theatrical career to date. So, again, why would that give me a 'vendetta' to 'strike out' at *you*, as you claim?"

Finally, I asked if he'd written such emails to all the other critics who panned his show. If so, I suggested, maybe he should spend less time attacking his critics and devote that energy to working on rewrites.

I ended by warning that I would pursue legal action if he continued trashing my character or tried to get me fired. I cc'd my lawyer, cc'd *Broads!*'s publicist, and cc'd Ryan at *WeHo News*.

I never heard another peep from Mr. Symon.

But the brouhaha was finally too much for Ryan. He eventually relented and added a disclaimer to the top of my *Broads!* review:

> "*WeHo News* encourages our readers to see the show themselves and make up their own minds."

I was astonished when I saw that. I quickly emailed Ryan, asking, "Why have a critic if you tell readers to see everything anyway?"

I reviewed a few more shows after that. But my heart just wasn't in it anymore. I found myself second-guessing my own reactions. Realizing I'd probably burned enough of those aforementioned bridges, I quit.

And now, to prove I can take it as well as dish it out, it's only fair to share how some critics have trashed me. Yes, I save the bad ones, too! Like I said, if you believe the good ones …

> "Acord indicates he may be capable of more with better material, but that's merely speculation"

Thus opined Dean Goodman in *Drama-Logue* of my San Francisco stage debut in the play *Happy Anniversary* by Lou Reda.

And my worst review ever?

Douglas W. Gordy of *The Slant* wrote of my performance in Tim Pinckney's *Message to Michael*:

> "…the comic timing hasn't quite gelled yet (particularly with lead actor Leon Acord – playing mousy Michael – who tends not to listen to his fellow actors, and whose performance thus seems overly-calculated [sic] and lacks spontaneity) …"

If I resisted sending a hateful email to *that* son of a bitch, Mr. Symon could've resisted writing to *this* son of a bitch!

# My First Plague

COVID? Terrifying. Monkeypox? Unnerving. But this isn't my first time at the rodeo.

In fact, I can barely remember a time before that *first* public-health scourge of my lifetime: AIDS.

I graduated high school in May 1981 at age 17. The day after graduation, I moved to Indianapolis to escape both farm life and parents not yet able to handle an openly gay son.

Compared to life on the farm, Indianapolis was the BIG CITY! When I got there, I was shocked not only to discover so many others like me – but that they were all having a helluva good time!

The summer of 1981. The last few months before the specter began to rise. Maybe it was the residual effects of the sexual revolution or the fading disco era. Or maybe it was because I was a naive former farm boy. But gay men were seemingly everywhere. They had their own neighborhoods, from "Homo Heights" uptown to "Faggot Flats" closer downtown. Businesses! Neighborhood societies!

Being out wasn't an "alternative lifestyle" in those days. It was punk. You were a walking, talking political statement. We were beginning to get some acceptance, but we were still a mysterious "Other" to most. Yes, sex was omnipresent. But it was about more in those post-Stonewall years. It was the realization that with self-acceptance came great freedom. Yes, some of us chose to celebrate at bars and bathhouses. And others of us opened art galleries, restaurants, started magazines, became designers, writers, actors. But marriage?

Why would we want to do something stupid like that? We were thrilled to be exempt from society's rules.

To the rest of the world, we knew how to be just quiet enough. We were still underground in most places, so we learned an unspoken code, a way of "knowing" when we found ourselves with our own kind.

To the straight urban crowd, we were chic. An asset at any party or office. Disco may be dead, but we were really beginning to thrive.

*New York Times,* July 1981:

> "Doctors in New York and California have diagnosed among homosexual men 41 cases of a rare and often rapidly fatal form of cancer. Eight of the victims died less than 24 months after the diagnosis was made."

I still remember my very first thought when I read that, flippant though it was. "Of course, gays can't just get some run-of-the-mill cancer! Oh, no! We have to get some 'rare, tropical disease!'"

The gay guys I knew dismissed it, if they gave it any thought at all. If they had heard about it at all. Few Hoosiers read the *New York Times*.

How many conversations during those next few months began with "Have you heard about this ... gay thing?" Yet almost all of the guys in my circle felt insulated from it – it was happening in New York and San Francisco. Nobody knew anyone *here* with this mystery disease.

Condoms? Hadn't entered the discussion. Safe sex? The term hadn't yet been coined. This disease didn't even have a name! Hell, the President of the United States refused to even address the crisis.

AYDS was still just an over-the-counter diet supplement. Can you imagine a time when someone might have actually said, "I'm gonna run down to the corner drug store to get pick me up some AYDS"?

Fall 1982. Joan Collins appears on the cover of *US* magazine. Along the top of the cover, a banner headline:

"*Mysterious Cancer That's Killing Gay Men*"

It was absurd, I thought. You can't "catch" cancer! I began to wonder, *maybe gay people* are *defective, maybe something in our DNA is unbalanced, and our bodies are breaking down.*

I wasn't the only one with a crazy theory.

"It's guys who use poppers! That's what causes it!"

"You only have to worry if you swallow."

"It's the government! They're testing a new biological weapon!"

And those were comments from the gay guys! Forget about the straight bigots and zealots who claimed it was a curse from God.

Yet, most guys in Indianapolis still thought they were safe.

By 1983, AIDS had a name. I had a new boyfriend. But in Indianapolis, safe sex still hadn't seemed necessary.

In 1984, we moved to San Francisco. There was no living in denial at Ground Zero. The homeless AIDS fighters living in a camp in the Civic Center. The zombies struggling to walk down Castro Street. The posters about safe sex in the subway stations. The seemingly endless obituaries in the *Bay Area Reporter*. For the first time in my life, AIDS seemed real. It was inescapable. And it was scary to be in a city where 75 percent of the men were believed to be HIV-positive.

But it was also almost comforting to live in a place where AIDS was on the front page of the newspaper, and opened the local news, almost every single day – without judgment.

My new boyfriend? He couldn't take it. Six months later, he moved back home. About a year later, he learned that being back in Indiana didn't make him safe. Two years after that, he was dead.

What would life be like if AIDS had never happened? I can't imagine. You bet I practice safe sex now. In fact, I'm wearing a condom as I write this!

On a personal note: Despite being openly gay, my parents never addressed my homosexuality after I came out. At most, my mom called it my "attitude" or being "that way." But I'm from Kokomo, Indiana – Ryan White's hometown. And when my aunt began raising money to have Ryan thrown out of school for having AIDS (which he contracted through a blood transfusion), my mom was incensed. She and I talked about AIDS for the first time. And that led to talking about being gay. And that eventually led to the totally cool parents I have today.

AIDS is no longer a death sentence. And it's hard to believe the advances I have seen in gay rights in my lifetime. We're living in a gay new world.

Those hundreds of thousands of men and women did not die in vain. They were the martyrs. Would gay marriage be a reality today if AIDS hadn't forced gay issues onto the nightly news? If gay men hadn't fought for the right to be at their lovers' sides? Would domestic partnership have evolved? AIDS humanized us in the eyes of many and reminded us of our own mortality. The party ends for everyone, eventually, no matter what.

But sometimes, I really do miss those early days, when we were more than an "alternative lifestyle." When being gay raised eyebrows. When we were the "Other."

When we were punk.

# A Twisted Vein

I somehow arrived at middle-age without ever breaking a bone, having surgery, or spending a night as a patient in a hospital. Pretty good, huh?

Especially considering my childhood was filled with jumping off barns, riding horses and mini-motorbikes, and working on a farm!

That is not to say my life has been free of scary medical-show drama.

Around 2003, I began to notice, while reading, that text was becoming a little blurry. I attributed it to my age (40 at the time), and mentally made a note to buy some reading glasses. I also noticed colors on TV became muted when I closed my left eye. Again, I assumed it was just a case of aging eyes.

Then one day, as I was walking to work in San Francisco's Financial District, I looked up at a high-rise building.

Is that building bulging? I wondered.

I closed my left eye. The building did, indeed, appear to have a small bulge – one or two floors warping outwards.

*How is that possible?*

I quickly made an appointment with my regular eye doctor, a wonderful woman named Dr. Christine Brischer.

As we sat down, I explained to her what I was experiencing. She looked into my left eye with her lighted pen, then my right. Then, without a word to me, she spun around in her chair, picked up the phone, and called a leading ophthalmologist.

"Hi, its Christine. I have a patient who needs to see you immediately. Can he come this afternoon? Good." The seriousness of her tone shook me to the bone.

She hung up, then spun around to face me.

"I hope you have good insurance," she said cryptically. "This is going to be very expensive."

She explained there was blood gathering behind my retina that required *immediate* treatment.

I left her office in a daze and immediately called Laurence. He left work early and joined me at the ophthalmologist's office.

After a thorough and grueling examination, the specialist explained what was going on. A small artery behind the center of my right retina had sprung a leak. The blood that was spilling out was pushing the retina forward, thus causing vision in that eye to appear warped.

The ophthalmologist conferred with his team. They suggested urgency. Considering the leak was located directly in the center of my eye, they recommended the "big guns" – a "hot" laser eye surgery. It would leave me with a permanent blind spot in the middle of my right eye, but the heat from the laser might – just might – seal up the leaky vein. We agreed.

My head was strapped into a chair. I was warned against moving for the 60 seconds or so that the laser was shooting into my eye, as the laser would burn (and blind) anything it touched.

The terrifying procedure began, and the entire time, I wondered *What if I have to sneeze? What if there's an earthquake? What if I fart?*

I didn't, there wasn't, and I didn't.

I was playing the villain in the play *Worse Than Chocolate* at the time. I assured director Jeffrey I'd recover sufficiently in time to return to the show following the mid-week break in performances. And I did, despite incredibly distracting "halos" that stage lighting caused in my recovering eye.[26]

That weekend, during a performance, as I'm "firing" Jaeson Post and demanding the office key from him, he dropped it as he handed it to me. I looked down. With my impaired vision, the brass-colored metal key vanished against the similarly colored wooden floor.

I looked at Jaeson. Rightfully remaining in character, he refused to pick it up.

I got on my hands and knees and felt for the keys with my hands, like a young, manic Patty-Duke-as-Helen-Keller. The audience actually loved it, loved seeing the heavy of the show (me) reduced to crawling on his hands and knees after being such a prick. It was a very scary moment which I think I pulled off.

We returned to the doctor for a follow-up a week later. I was less than delighted to learn the vein was still leaking. So now, I had increasingly warped vision *plus* a blind spot right in the center of my eye (which they explained would expand as

---

[26] I should've worn the eye patch I'd been sporting after the surgery, but critics already felt my villain was a little too over-the-top!

years went by). I began to question the wisdom of using the "big guns" right away.

The doctor suggested we try the hot laser again. But one blind spot is enough, thank you very much. So, we opted for the less-powerful option: they injected me full of photo-sensitive chemicals then shot a "cold" laser at the leak. Then I hid from direct sunlight for the next three days (not so easy to do in Los Angeles), as the chemicals would leave me susceptible to serious sunburn within minutes.

That procedure didn't stop the leak either. So, we tried it again. Then again.

After seven more expensive cold laser surgeries over 18 months, the leak was finally – *finally* – cauterized.

But what the hell had caused the vein to pop a leak in the first place? That question left the various eye professionals stymied.

Over a year later, while I was still undergoing unsuccessful laser treatments, we consulted with a vision specialist at the University of California at San Francisco.

"Did you grow up on a farm?" he asked within moments.

"Why, yes, I did. Why?"

"Histoplasmosis," he answered, explaining the infection – caused by inhaling dried bird droppings – is common in people who live(d) on midwestern farms. Most people carry it without ever developing symptoms.

Yes, as a matter of fact, I even spent a few months as a kid one summer raising chickens and selling the eggs to neighbors and family members. And I remembered, Mom had battled the same thing when I was a young kid – in her case, it attacked the veins in her legs, putting her in a wheelchair for a week or two.

Over the years, my blind spot from that hot laser has continued to grow, basically leaving me effectively blind in the center of my right eye. If I live long enough, the slowly expanding blind spot will eventually leave me legally blind in that eye.

I've gotten used to it. The human eye is an amazing thing. It fills in blind spots with the colors surrounding it. I really only feel impaired when taking a conventional vision test, or while watching a 3D or IMAX movie, or if I'm driving in an unfamiliar part of town after dark.

The plus side? I have to submit to thorough, rigorous eye exams every year to ensure the leak doesn't reopen.

How is that a "plus," you ask?

Most of the patients of my ophthalmologist are elderly men and women battling macular degeneration, so every time I show up for an appointment, I enjoy the increasingly rare sensation of being the youngest person in the room – a feat I rarely accomplish in LA!

Or anywhere else these days, now that I think about it...

# Am I a "They"?

About two decades ago, while shooting the film *Foucault WHO?,* director Jed Bell made a casual observation.

"You kinda like girly clothes, don't you?" he asked me one day, as I arrived on set in a rather fabulous retro black-and-green sweater.

I wasn't offended or even taken aback. Because I knew the answer was – and is – "yes, I guess I do."

I could blame it on being a young adult in the 1980s. Big, blousy shirts. Short sleeves that went all the way down to the elbow. Deep V-necks. Pleated pants. Double-breasted jackets. Shoulder pads. Never before that decade of excess (or since) has there been such variety in men's wear. And thanks to MTV, androgyny had never been more popular.

But the truth is, I'd always preferred clothes that had just a little bit more flair and frills, more style, than most guys.

I've also always preferred having long hair, because I just don't really feel like myself with short hair.

Until recently, I accepted my personal preferences as just that. I've always accepted that I am made up of both male and female energy. I considered myself a "Nancy," a.k.a. a slightly effeminate male, and I never gave it much thought beyond that.

But these days, I have to ask myself.

"Am I really a 'they'?"

There's a lot to unpack here.

I was subconsciously aware, almost since birth, that my fearless, rough-and-tumble older sister Tammy was more like the son Dad always wanted, while sensitive, delicate little me was more akin to the daughter Mom always hoped to have.

Around age 5, I went through a week-long phase of being extremely attached to one of Mom's purses. (To my parents' credit, they never made a big deal out of it.) I didn't carry it in public because, even at that early age, I knew that would be flirting with disaster. But at home, it rarely left my side for several days.

I played with my sister's Barbie dolls. I hated G.I. Joe and trucks and toy guns.

I loved horses, books, climbing trees, and talking to myself as I strolled barefoot through the country.

I carried my books against my chest (like girls) and not against my hip (like boys).

One day, in third grade, Dad picked me up from school. I excitedly began to tell him about my day.

"So, another girl in class said that – "

Dad immediately interrupted me.

"Another *girl?*" he asked.

"Oh, I just mean, another student in class! Who's a girl!" I stammered.

But did I?

I didn't play "war" with classmates, nor "cops and robbers," nor "cowboys and Indians." We played *Star Trek*, and I usually pretended to be Lt. Uhura.

I hated any kind of sport. I was the last one picked for dodgeball, and the first one knocked out of the game. I spent most of P.E. class in the outfield, like Charlie Brown, praying nobody would hit the ball that far (and they always did). Shop class was an ordeal.

My physicality was also a problem. Despite growing up on a farm, my physiology made it impossible for me to gain muscle mass. Instead of developing a masculine swagger, my walk could only be described as a girlish gait. Being tall and very skinny merely accentuated my swishy-ness.

I was terribly embarrassed by the lumps that eventually came with being an adolescent male. I worked to keep everything pointed downwards, so as to not create any bulges. Was I trying to look female? Was I disgusted with my junk, ashamed to be a male? Or was I simply mortified that my "pee pee," which until recently was only good for urination purposes, had taken on an apparent, unpredictable life of its own?

I'm still not sure what the answer is.

As an adult, I felt uncomfortable using the word "man" to describe myself. (I still do.) "Guy" was okay. So was "dude." But "man"? That word carried lots of masculine baggage that I didn't feel I could live up to. That I didn't *want* to live up to.

On the flip side, the few times I dressed up in drag weren't really that fun, either.

So, am I a "they" or what?

The gay-rights movement took over 50 years to achieve marriage equality. Comparatively, it may seem to some that the trans-rights movement happened overnight. But that's simply not true.

I knew trans folks way back in the early 1980s, when I worked at an Indianapolis drag bar playing "male lead" (oh, the irony). Back then, they were called "transsexuals," but my fellow entertainers certainly weren't the first. Christine Jorgensen and Renee Richards famously blazed trails long before Indy's Rochelle Lamar, Foxy Roxy, and Leslie Ryan.

Director Jed Bell, writer/actor Jaeson Post, cabaret star Veronica Klaus, and actors Quinn Fontaine and Stanly Crass, are a few of the transgender folk I've worked with in my "legit" career.

These days, between social media's omnipresence, and the GOP's willingness to "weapon-ize" differences to fuel their ridiculously divisive "culture wars," gender issues now have a blinding-white spotlight shining on them. It's easy to mistakenly believe that the push for trans rights is a relatively new phenomenon.

But they have always been around.

Sadly, I've recently lost friendships due to transphobia. While I understand why some women feel that that a ladies' room should be a "penis-free zone," I find their alarm to be more than a bit hysterical.

Why? Because I've been going to men's rooms for over 50 years and I've not once seen someone else's penis – not even in the men's room at a gay bar!

So why would a *trans woman* run around a ladies' room with a dick flopping out when she wants you to see and accept her as a woman?

Yes, some kids really *do* know, from a very early age, that their identity doesn't line up with their genitalia. For them, it's about more than clothes or hair or purses, or feeling like they are a combo pack of both genders. For some, the feeling of having been born in the wrong body is undeniable.

That said, some kids *do* go through phases. And it's up to mom and dad to be able to tell the difference, as hard as that can be.

Long story short, in my opinion, nobody should make a life-long decision before they get a driver's license. So parents must listen, be open and flexible, get therapists involved (for both their kid and themselves) if necessary, and take their kid's journey with them.

All without judgment.

Thank God I never had children.


I will always support my trans brothers and sisters in their battles. Because ultimately, we *all* benefit from their courage. They're breaking down ridiculous, outdated, and unnecessary notions of gender, such as what we can and can't wear, what job is or isn't appropriate, what hobbies are allowed or not.

Thanks to them, we can do away with the parts of ourselves that have been forced upon us by others, or by social pressure to conform. We can stop trying to be what we're *supposed* to be. And start being who we truly *are*.

So if you're a macho trucker who likes to do needlepoint, thank a trans person for lowering the stakes.

Isn't freedom ultimately a wonderful thing?


I digress. Back to my initial question. Am *I* a "they"?

I *am* somewhere between the strict gender lines, and often I actually do feel equal parts male *and* female – which, by definition, makes me "non-binary."

The answer is, "Yes. I am a 'they.'"

So, now what?

Perhaps if I were 20 or 30 years younger, I would embrace my "otherness," change my pronouns, stroke on some black nail polish, pull on a kilt, and "take a walk on the wild side."

But I would stop short of hormones or making physical changes.

Because, while I don't always feel 100% like a man, it's what I'm used to. I still prefer my penis to the magical, mysterious workings of the female. I guess I'll just stick to being a girly guy. A sissy. A Nancy. (It's still better than being a "Karen"!)

And let's face it, I'm probably a bit too old to make a radical lifestyle change now. At 60, I've marched in enough parades. I've provided enough shock. I've actually reached a point where I enjoy *not* always being the center of attention.

And quite frankly, haven't I put my parents through enough already?

# Sub-lebrity Auction

Many of them have done it. And if they haven't yet, chances are good they will eventually.

Once a celebrity reaches a certain age, or enjoys their greatest successes, or moves to smaller digs, or experiences a reversal of fortune, they'll auction off some prized possessions. As well as a lot of their junk. Clothing. Furniture. Mementos. Love letters. Knick-knacks and bric-a-brac. All available to the highest bidder.

It can be great fun if you're a fan of said celebrity. I spent many days in 2016, pouring over the Julian's Auctions' catalog of the Joan Collins auction. Alas, I couldn't afford to bid on a thing. At $100 each, I couldn't even afford the catalog! (Thank you, Lisa Vigil!)

It can also be a bit sad, as you realize these celebs are parting with some favorite memories and important parts of their past. You can't help but wonder, which pieces do they hate to part with? Which lots are they glad to dump off onto someone else?

Being a mere unknown, I'll never have the thrill of making money by selling my most precious crap to the world. It's not just obscurity that keeps me from selling my wares. It's the fact that, other than sentimental value, my most treasured items aren't worth shit!

But if I *were* a once-famous has been now offering his property to the highest bidder, my pathetic little catalog might look something like this:

### Lot 1: Joe Allen Ashtray (damaged)

Circa 1988, ceramic, paint, and glue. Damaged in 2022, poorly repaired with hot-glue gun, but contains too much sentimental value to discard. Purloined from the famous Manhattan theatre eatery during a trip to New York City to celebrate author's 25th birthday. Joe Allen can be seen in the 1981 film *Only When I Laugh*, author's favorite film, starring Marsha Mason. Not advised for use as an actual ashtray.

### Lot 2: Wonder Woman Statuette

Circa early 1990s, approximately 12-1/2 inches tall; ceramic and various paints, both glossy and matte. An early gift to author from Laurence Whiting during the early days of their relationship. Assembled and (badly) painted (and repainted, and repainted) by the author.

(*See* Lots 8 and 9 for more Wonder Woman items.)

## Lot 3: Books & Recordings by and About Quentin Crisp (two autographed)

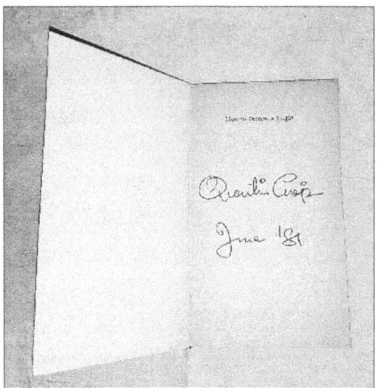

Lot of hardcover and paperback books, audio cassette tapes, DVDs, VHS tapes, circa various. Utilized by author to research Quentin Crisp for the play *Carved in Stone* (2002, 2009). Collection includes several titles written by Crisp (*Naked Civil Servant, How to Be a Virgin, How to Have a Lifestyle*) as well as several books about Crisp, including *The Stately Homo* and the biography *Quentin Crisp: The Profession of Being* by Nigel Kelly, which includes a photo of author as Quentin Crisp and a brief description of the play *Carved in Stone*, and signed by Kelly. Includes one DVD of the documentary feature film *Resident Alien* featuring Crisp during his New York years in the 1980s. *How to be a Virgin* and *Naked Civil Servant* are signed by Crisp.

## Lot 4: Salt & Pepper/Sugar Bowl Set

Circa early 1960s, ceramic set manufactured by Artmark Associates. Missing sugar spoon/ladle. Originally owned by author's mother, this set of salt & pepper shakers in the shape of bears, and a sugar bowl in the shape of a tree trunk (with small "squirrel" as handle), fascinated author as a young boy. Gifted to him from his mother since he has fawned over it during every visit to his parents' home ever since.

## Lot 5: Dad's Flight Log

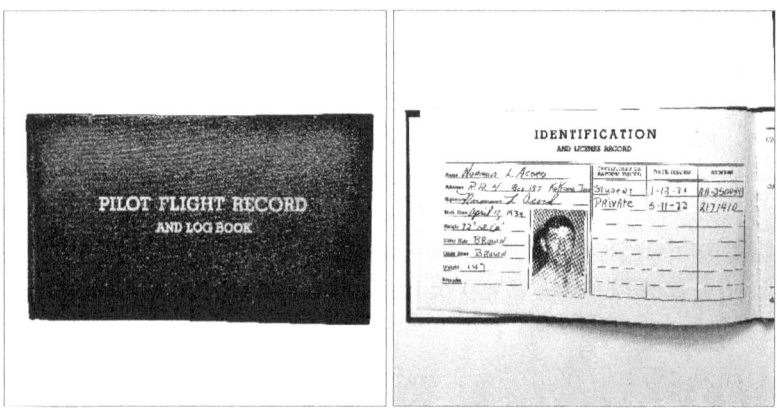

Circa early 1970s. Flight log gifted to author from his father. Author's endlessly ambitious father earned his private pilot's license and terrorized author as a young child by pretending the plane's engine had stopped during flights. (Any wonder author frequently feels like a failure when comparing himself to his pop?)

### Lot 6: Black Patent-Leather Boots

Circa early 2010s, patent leather with rubber soles, cotton shoelaces, ankle high, size 11. Purchased from "JackHammer.com" clothing website (long since deceased). If you've seen the author at any public appearance in the past 15 years, chances are good you've seen him in these, as 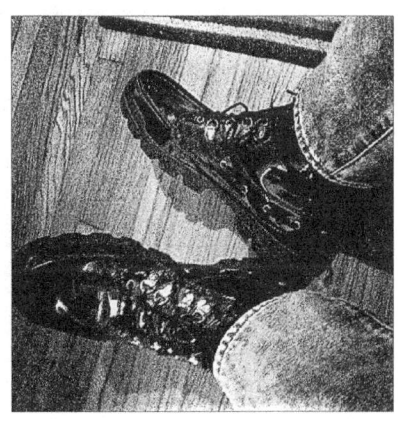 they remain his favorite pair of shoes to date. Alas, slightly damaged from overuse, left foot now has small tear on the left side.

### Lot 7: Collection of Old Cell Phones

Circa various. Collection of discarded, outdated cellphones that author can't seem to part with. No longer operational, but still includes data for the truly inspired. Includes deep-red Blackberry which author referred to as his "Raspberry" and was seen in the second season of *Old Dogs & New Tricks.*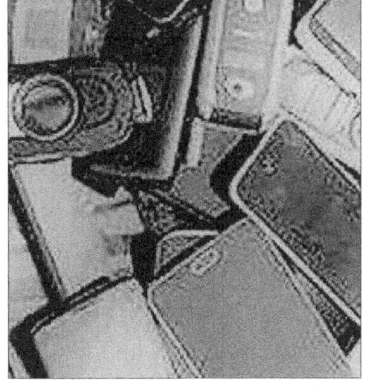

## Lot 8: Wonder Woman Wall Hanging

Circa 1973, 20"x16", glass, metal, pressboard, and paint. Classic golden-age Wonder Woman logo and figure painted on glass, so as to appear "flying over" full-color 1940s-era comic-book pages matted beneath. Extremely fragile. Buyer takes full responsibility for safe transport after sale. No refunds offered.

## Lot 9: Collection of Wonder Woman Action Figures/Figurines/Toys

Circa various, plastic and fabrics. Assortment of various Wonder Woman action figures and toys collected by and/or gifted to the author as an adult. Author's collection was previously massive but mostly sold off in various purges to pay for multiple theatrical endeavors. These favorite figures survived. (Tall ceramic statute sold separately; *see* Lot #2.)

### Lot 10: Collection of Homemade Bracelets

Lot of 10 bracelets, circa 2020s, various materials (mostly cheap). Collection of bracelets designed and created by the author during a "let's make jewelry!" phase. Shoddily made. No warranties offered. Could fall apart at any moment.

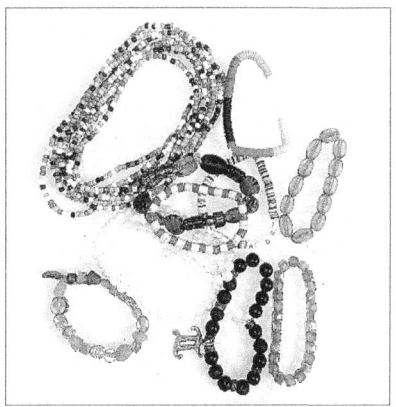

### Lot 11: Jan Hooks' Telephone

Circa unknown. AT&T "slim line" phone gifted to author by actor Wenzel Jones, after Jones learned of author's fanatical devotion to actress Jan Hooks (1957-2014), the late *Saturday Night Live* star of the 1990s. (Author has no knowledge of how telephone came into Jones' possession.)

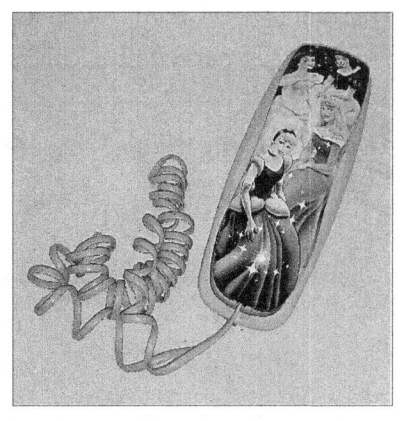

Pink, and adorned with image of various Disney princesses. Author assumes it still works (but who has a landline anymore?).

## Lot 12: Collection of Original Motion-Picture Soundtracks and Broadway Cast Recordings

Lot of approximately 25 "albums," circa 1970s-1990s, vinyl and cardboard. Various motion-picture soundtracks, including *Superman*, *Star Wars*, *Foul Play*, *King Kong* (1976), and Broadway original-cast recordings, including *Woman of the Year*, *Applause*, *Goldilocks*, *Guys & Dolls*, *A Chorus Line*. In extremely poor condition from spending weeks at a time out of their sleeves on the floor of the author's teenaged bedroom. Not responsible for needle damage from scratches, cracks and crevices. Author's mother *not* a fan, particularly of *King Kong* soundtrack ("Turn that down, it's making me nervous!"). Sold extremely "as is."

## Lot 13: Collection of "Readers" Eyeglasses

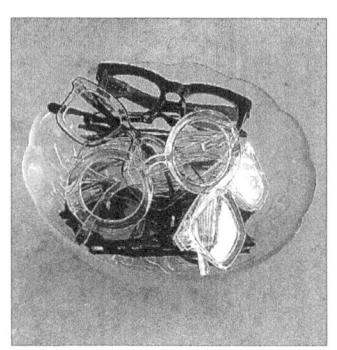

Circa 2020s, plastic. Collection of 15 or so eyeglasses for reading, 1.5 magnification strength. Manufactured by eyekeepers.com, for which author was briefly a "brand ambassador." Range/variety of frame styles can be described as "from Clark Kent to Elaine Stritch."

## Lot 14: Black/Gray Sequined Jacket

Circa 2018, polyester and black and gray sequins. Manufactured by Suslo Couture. Size L-42. Worn by author in front-cover photograph of memoir *SUB-LEBRITY* (published 2020). Loved by the author but, honestly, how often (and where) could he *ever* wear this again? Lot includes autographed copy of said book.

## Lot 15: Prop American Express "Black" Credit Card

Circa 2014, this faux credit card, created by amazing designer Danielle Lee, was used by author's "Nathan Adler" character in the "All About (X'mas) Eve" episode of *Old Dogs & New Tricks*. Not to be used for actual purchases. (Author will not bail you out if you do!)

Which lots are treasures? Which are trash? I'll let you speculate.

Oh, and I reserve the right to change my mind should I ever find myself in desperate need or decide to raise money for a new producing project. (But until then, don't call or email me asking for discounts!)

# Worry *and* Be Happy!

Like most everyone else in the free world, I was devastated to learn of actor Leslie Jordan's death in a car accident in October 2022. Such a positive life force. Such a fearless talent. Such a funny man.

The news of his death threatened to send me spiraling into despair because I was dealing with some scary family drama at the time, as well as overdosing on predictions of mid-term gloom and doom on MSNBC.[27]

I also found his death to be triggering because he had long reminded me of my good friend Jeffrey Hartgraves, a similarly talented man who was also taken from us too soon.

But just as I was falling into a bottomless depression, I stumbled upon the following quote from Mr. Jordan on social media:

> "Happiness is a choice. Happiness is a habit. And happiness is something you have to work hard at. It does not just happen."

Now, I've heard variations on this philosophy before. My hubby is a devotee of the late Louise Hay, whose message, in

---

[27] Which, fortunately, turned out to be a false alarm – this time!

a nutshell, boils down to "the thoughts we think, and the words we speak, create our reality."

She didn't lie. Alas, Ms. Hay always struck me as a little too *la-de-da*, *airy-fairy* to take seriously. After all, it's hard (for me) to take that kind of advice from the head of a multi-million-dollar publishing outfit.

But seeing that quote from Mr. Jordan hit me differently, and hard. He had had a difficult life. Growing up gay and effeminate in the Deep South. Addiction to booze and drugs. Multiple arrests.

Often, very funny people become very funny as the result of very painful anguish. (*See* Robin Williams.)

So coming from Mr. Jordan, this advice had real power.

It's easy to assume that, once an actor is successful, he or she (or they) waves goodbye to personal pain and sends their demons packing. But that is not the case. And let's be honest, even if you're successful, there are easier things to be in the gay world than short, old, and nelly!

To be sure, Mr. Jordan must have had private moments of doubt, fear, anger, regret. We all do. The challenge – the "hard work" – is finding your happiness despite all the negative emotions, all the bad news, all the challenges of real life.

I needed to receive his message. For far too long, I've let my life be defined by the things that piss me off, or problems I needed to fix, or goals I hadn't reached. I'd let a negative comment on Facebook stick in my craw and ruin my mood for hours. I'd watch reports of how MAGA Republicans are trying to murder democracy, and I would fly into a rage – and stay there all day.

How do we acknowledge the bad news, the hard knocks life throws our way, yet still manage to be happy? Is it "living in denial" to find joy when there's so much to feel unhappy about? Do we have to become unthinking Pollyannas to pull it off?

No. That's where the "hard work" from Mr. Jordan's quote comes in.

The truth is, we all can and do feel more than one emotion at the same time. But we have to make the effort.

I write in my journal every morning. Many mornings, I also scribbled out a quick "gratitude list" of things in my life that I appreciated.

I no longer list my sources of gratitude. That's a passive exercise. Yes, I would acknowledge the good, write it down – but then I would forget about it. And often, I found myself writing down the same items each morning by rote. (*"My parents. Laurence. Our cat Toby. Old Dogs & New Tricks."*) I felt gratitude in the moment, but it never stuck.

These days, after I've made my diary entry, I sometimes write a list of moments that made me feel *happy*, instead of things for which I'm grateful. The good things in my life that bring a smile, or warm my heart, or make me laugh.

It's a much more active exercise.

For example, I'd write "Our cat Toby" on my gratitude list. Okay. But what about that little guy makes me happy? The way he wails when he hears us at the front door! The way he cuddles in bed for belly rubs before the sun comes up! The way he arches his back and does his "scary kitty dance" when he gets really excited!

Having created and starred in a hit streaming TV series doesn't really make me happy anymore – especially since it was almost a decade ago. It's becoming a distant memory. So now I list "that lovely note from the new viewer" or "laughing over brunch with Amanda," (whom I cast as my loyal assistant "Lydia") or "getting a small royalty payment from Amazon Prime."

"Laurence" has been replaced on the list by items like, "Laurence's homemade chocolate milkshakes," for example, or "when Laurence and I laugh together at a good joke."

Instead of just writing "my parents," I list the times we've shared – specific moments – that make me happy. "Making Dad laugh." "Holding Mom's hand."

Thinking of those actions actually *ignites* happiness within me – much more happiness than simply acknowledging that these people and things merely exist. These are moving images and active memories that I can pull up like flashcards when I'm feeling less than joyous.

Those flashcards don't eliminate fear and anxiety. They don't change what's happening in the "outside world." But it's good to remind myself that there's more to life than just negative emotions and bad news. There's more to do in life than just *react*.

Another tool I'm utilizing these days to consistently brighten my mood is music. To quote William Congreve, "Music hath charms to soothe the savage breast. To soften rocks or bend the knotted oak." It certainly has the power to lighten my spirits!

These days, if I'm in my car – and as I live in LA, I'm in my car a lot – I have music blasting instead of news. Soundtracks, Prince, Bowie, Blondie, Harry Styles, disco. Whatever it takes to get me humming a tune as I reach my destination.

Some days, I just feel too damned sour to pick music to play. It's those days when I need it the most, so I'll force myself to open Spotify despite my mood. And within minutes, I've gone from sour to sweet. Or at least to sweeter than sour!

Mr. Jordan was right. Unless you're really lucky, or slightly brain damaged, happiness does not just happen. Not in today's crazy world.

Instead of expecting the world to make us happy, and being miserable when it fails to deliver, we need to take the reins to our moods. Staying positive and upbeat is a DIY gig.

It's a lesson I needed to learn. As I face the physical challenges of getting older, as my family ages, and as we watch America lurch dangerously close to fascism, I'm still struggling against turning into a grumpy old queen.

But who knows? If I'm able to keep this up, maybe my *next* book will be *less* grumpy!

Thank you, Mr. Jordan.

## Special Thanks

The term "self-publishing" is a bit of a misnomer, as it implies the author did it all on his, her, or their own. Truth is, this book would not exist without the help of some very good friends, some wonderful family, and one great love.

Deep thanks & undying gratitude to my *de facto* editors **Courtney Flavin** and **Jenn Garagliano** for putting in Oxford commas, taking out taking superfluous exclamation points, being brutally honest when needed, and committing the time required to make me a much better writer than I am.

**Danielle "Lovey" Mazer** suggested this book's title after patiently listening to me prattle off maybe a dozen other possible names – and I love her all the more for it!

**Lisette & Norman A. Palley** are the world's best in-laws, for providing love & support, photos, and a quiet place (and technical know-how) to record the audio book.

Much appreciation to my beloved *Old Dogs & New Tricks* colleague **Curt Bonnem** for providing a crash course on audio-book production and narration to this first timer.

Thank you to busy Hollywood scenic designer and friend **Alan Jergens** for providing artistic & photographic assistance for no more than a pack of beer!

I'm indebted to my "alpha readers" **Mac McCormick**, **Eddie Ruggario**, **Sally Patton**, and **Lisa Lipscomb-Robinson** for catching typos, raising clarity questions, "voting" on draft covers, and playing cheerleaders as this book inched to completion. Thank you to each and every one of you.

And much love and appreciation, as always, for my wonderful husband **Laurence Whiting** and his unwavering encouragement and blind faith.

Photo: Norman A. Palley

## About the Author

**Leon Acord** is an actor, writer, occasional producer, and recovering nicotine addict. His 2020 memoir *SUB-LEBRITY* was a five-star Amazon bestseller. He created, wrote, and starred as "Nathan Adler" in the hit streaming TV series *Old Dogs & New Tricks* (2011-2016, Prime Video). Leon has appeared in numerous film and theatrical productions, including portraying Quentin Crisp in two productions of Jeffrey Hartgraves' stage hit *Carved in Stone*, and lead roles in the West Coast premieres of *Message to Michael*, *Last Sunday in June*, *Dreamboy,* and *Thief River* at New Conservatory Theatre Center in San Francisco. In Los Angeles, he's appeared in the world premieres of the plays *Scheme of Things* and *Salsa Saved the Girls*, and twice played the Ghost of Jacob Marley in *gay apparel: A Christmas Carol*. He's appeared in feature films *Some Prefer Cake*, *Final Remains*, *Hot Guys with Guns*, and *OPEN*, to name a few, and in dozens of short films, including film-fest favs *Deer Season*, *Foucault WHO?* and *aWake*. He wrote his one-man show *Last Sunday in June* (1997) and co-authored the 2015 play *Setting the Record Gay*, in which he played (gulp) himself. His writings have appeared on Huffington Post, and in *Back Stage*, *San Francisco Examiner*, and the journal *Human Prospect*. He lives in Culver City with husband Laurence Whiting and their cat Toby. www.LeonAcord.com

Made in the USA
Monee, IL
05 June 2023